HOW DID WE GET HERE?

HOW DID WE GET HERE?

A girl's guide to finding herself

MPOOMY LEDWABA

Jonathan Ball Publishers

JOHANNESBURG · CAPE TOWN

© Text: Nompumelelo Ledwaba (2024)
© Cover image: Katlego Mokubyane, New Katz Studio (2024)
© Published edition: Jonathan Ball Publishers (2024)

First published in South Africa in 2024 by
JONATHAN BALL PUBLISHERS
A division of Media24 (Pty) Ltd
PO Box 33977
Jeppestown
2043

ISBN 978-1-77619-386-8
Hardcover ISBN 978-1-77619-453-7
ebook ISBN 978-1-77619-387-5
audiobook ISBN 978-1-77619-448-3

*Every effort has been made to trace the copyright holders and to obtain
their permission for the use of copyright material. The publishers apologise
for any errors or omissions and would be grateful to be notified of any
corrections that should be incorporated in future editions of this book.*

jonathanball.co.za
x.com/JonathanBallPub
facebook.com/JonathanBallPublishers

Cover by Melanie Kriel
Design and typesetting by Melanie Kriel
Set in Bembo Std

MaNdlovu, you never learnt to read or write, yet your intelligence, wisdom and knowledge of God's word have been passed on and, because of you, I get to write a book. uNobelungu unencwadi, Gogo.

My grandmother Agnes, your resilience and desire for more are stitched into my being. You model a woman in leadership, a woman of class and a woman who has broken every barrier set for her.

Nomsa, Angela Mondlane, the woman who spoke success into my life before I even set foot on earth. You hold space for every part of me, without judgement but with a love that knows no bounds. You know me at my best and at my worst, yet you still love me like a newborn baby who has done no harm.

Nuri, Lethabo Ledwaba, my little light and joy. May this book give you a glimpse of who you come from and the wings to go as far as God desires. A born leader, creative and lover of life.

To you, my dear reader, my gal pal, I give you permission to heal.

⚠ CONTENT INCLUDES REFERENCES TO SUICIDE AND SEXUAL ASSAULT.

Contents

Introduction

That dictionary has finally paid off.

Thanks, Mom.

I am a storyteller, and it's how I make a living. Though I did not always know that, it's pretty clear to me now. How does the Oxford fit into this, you may ask? Well, I come from a family of educators, on my mother's side. I am a university dropout but these days I, too, consider myself a teacher. Not in the orthodox way, but the Sunday newsletter I write for my community, for example, might leave you with some homework – such as the '5 conversation starters' I offered on Mother's Day – and my podcast might list a few points for you to consider implementing.

'MO-O-O-M!' Shouting from the living room. 'How do you spell "because"?'

While whipping up a chicken stew and cabbage, or uphuthu, depending on how tired she was from a full day of teaching the Queen's English at a Zulu school, my mother would yell back: 'Mpumi, thatha idictionary.' This was the foundation of my relationship with words and hard work.

As you flip through the pages of my life, you might be surprised by a few things, you might totally relate to some, you might side-eye me for some of my views or you might find yourself giggling as they open the door to your own weird thoughts, depending on who you are. In any case, I want to invite you into my home and into my space – I'd like us to take this journey together. Think of it as a date with that gal pal you know from social media, whom you totally vibe with online, but whom you are not really sure you could be friends with in real life. As I cosy up in front of my fireplace with the sound of rain falling outside, I let you in on who I am, what has happened to me and how I got to 30 and to Wisdom & Wellness. The good, the scary, the messy and of course the lessons – and, finally, the love and acceptance of … me!

As you explore how I achieved so much so soon (sometimes overachieving, to my detriment), you will understand why that Oxford dictionary was instrumental in bringing about a little girl who committed to a life of doing hard things and, more recently, addressing the elephant in the room!

And what better way to share more of myself than in a good old-fashioned book? There is something about time and effort devoted to pages that results in a greater sense of reward … kind of like when I searched for, and finally found, 'xylophone' in the dictionary and thereafter never forgot how to spell it. Well, you are about to find out that I grew tired of being a black girl doing well in life and apologising for it. Minimising my experiences, my pain, my hurt and my frustrations because someone else has it worse. As true as that is, my experience matters too, and I didn't reach this point by chance … And I can finally say it.

Make yourself comfortable and join me as I tell all on how we got here.

Prologue

My name is Nompumelelo, which means 'mother of success' in isiZulu.

My mother named me, and I believe it was the first prophecy of my life.

I have lived my life knowing that everything I do is predicated on my name.

I believe that a big part of my life's purpose is to birth success and share it with others. Not just material success but holistic success.

My paternal grandmother, MaNdlovu, called me Nobelungu, which in literal terms means 'white lady'. This has to do not with the colour of my skin but with demeanour, presence and attitude. In her day, only white women had authority, confidence and flair, and that's what my grandmother was referring to – a 'boss lady'. She named me thus because, growing up, I was demanding and assertive, I took up space. I still do.

I carry myself in accordance with the names I was given by the women who birthed me.

Does that mean I have everything figured out?

Not at all.

I am a work in progress.

PART ONE
I know that
I was loved

1

The elephant
in the room

It will always be awkward, meeting strangers who greet me on a
random Tuesday looking crusty at my local Woolies.

'Mommy, how do they know your name?' Nuri asks, sharing
my confusion.

That's it, that's what got me here: introducing myself and telling
the story of how so many people know who I am. My story.

'Hi, I'm Mpoomy Ledwaba.'

I was born Nompumelelo Amanda Mondlane, but my family
have always called me Mpumi, and I used Amanda at school because I couldn't stand the white teachers fumbling my very simple
name. (PSA: if you can say Eloise, you can say Mpumi.)

And now I am Mpoomy Ledwaba to most. It started when I
registered an account on the socials aeons ago and was inspired
by my cool aunt, Busi. She changed her name to Boocy in her
high school days. I thought she was the best thing since sliced
bread so, naturally, I wanted to be like her, dress like her, write like
her and even change my name to resemble hers. When I finally

got to choose my name when registering my Twitter account, it was my time to shine – as Mpoomy. In 2017, my husband, who goes by Brenden Praise as his stage name, gave me the surname Ledwaba. Mpoomy Ledwaba rolls off the tongue like the taste of the first sip of my oat milk cappuccino … pretty smooth. (I'm drinking one as I write this.)

I was born in January, the first baby Nomsa and Godfrey Mondlane had together. I always got special treatment at my grandmother's house because I was 'Godi's' child – that's what my family affectionately calls my dad. But in the month of Januworry, when everyone is broke after Christmas, birthday presents and big parties are not a thing. I got those only on my 13th, 16th and 21st birthdays. The continual excuse of it being the beginning of the year so no money became tiring, and eventually I managed my expectations to avoid disappointment. I must admit, I expected a few more gifts for my 30th, but not much has changed. So I work hard and buy myself all the things I love; most importantly, I give myself every experience I feel I deserve.

I come from a very big family on both sides. My mom has three siblings. My dad has about 11, who have at least five children each. When I say 11, I can't be absolutely sure, there could be more. You know what our families are like. Just when you least expect it – often at a funeral – a new cousin or brother will turn up. Which brings me to my brothers and sisters. I thought I had four siblings; it turns out I have five – we recently discovered a 16-year-old brother. All these siblings make me a middle child of sorts, but I don't have even a whiff of middle child syndrome (whatever that is). If anything, I have firstborn syndrome, perhaps because I am my mother's firstborn.

I have an older sister, Lindokuhle, whom we affectionately call Tunky. She is well on her way to 40. Okay, she is 36. And she is followed by my brother Andrew. (Vusi is his first name, but he hates it and always introduces himself as Andrew.) We call him Tough Guy because apparently he was pretty big, and tough, as a baby. Most people get his name wrong, calling him Big Guy or Tough Man or other weird combinations. He is 34. These numbers sound very adulty, considering that I played with these people as kids. Tunky and Tough Guy have the same mom. Then comes *meee*. You have more than 200 pages to learn all you need to know about me. Probably more than you bargained for!

Right after me is my little sister, Nontobeko. Nonto recently had her first baby, who is pretty much *my* baby. I'm not afraid to admit that it's favouritism: he is my most loved person in the family right now. Nonto is also a January child, and I make it a point to send her money for her birthday because I know how much those birthdays can suck. She's 26, very laid-back and absolutely hilarious. She does the best Nigerian and Zimbabwean accent impressions, and laughs in the middle of tense situations. If you ever cry in front of her, she gets so awkward you just have to pull yourself together. But I love that about her.

Then there is the baby of the family, who ironically is the tallest and largest of us: Mtho, better known as Uncle Jack. We woke up one day to hear him calling himself Jack, and that's who he's been ever since. He may not realise just how gifted he is, but I see it: now 24, he's athletic, musical and confident, and everyone likes him. He had bad eczema growing up. We used to love tickling him as a baby; he would turn bright red, and my dad would yell, 'Don't tickle him too much, he will die!' with a straight face. What? Die from tickling? That's how we knew he was the favourite.

We are all very different and complicated, but we love each other, and sometimes that's enough.

Writing a book about yourself at the age of 30 may seem crazy. It certainly seemed crazy to me at first. But when I thought about it I realised something: I've always been a storyteller, I just didn't know that my stories could or would take the form of a book. Or maybe I did, but it was one of those silent dreams you couldn't mention to a soul because it was so big and audacious, and how dared I even think I could do something like that? For as long as I can remember, my life has revolved around books, talking and being on stage. I never got less than 90 per cent for my creative writing exams, and every English teacher I ever had affirmed my writing skills. I even created a magazine using Microsoft Word on my dad's computer. I thought it was easy, that everybody could do it. I mean, you just have to make stories up. But it turns out it doesn't come as naturally to others. I worked in the school library during second break and enjoyed reading *The Princess Diaries* series on the job, but I got removed from that esteemed position because I talked too much. I love reading, but I love talking more!

I realised that I wanted to write a book around 2021. Having undergone extensive therapy and immersing myself in my health and wellness journey, I came to understand that my experiences were not unique. Many people never get the chance to process what has happened to them, what has shaped them, and how they respond to the world and to people around them. This process was crucial to my healing. I fixated on becoming a better version of myself, and I wanted to share my transformative journey. One random day while out on a run (where I often get my best ideas), I felt as though I was personally called by God to do it. At the time, on my YouTube channel I would cook while telling stories. Similarly, for my book the idea was to gather recipes from my childhood and pair them with some wisdom and a few stories from my life.

Brenden happened to be reversing out of our driveway when I returned home. Sweating and panting, I hopped into his car and began to babble, my mind functioning faster than I could get the words out. 'I'm writing a cookbook, but with stories of wisdom!' 'Uh, that's great! But is that really the book you want to write?' He did not shy away from questioning my intentions. Admittedly, he had a point. I probably will create a cookbook with stories one day, but this one had to come first. I shied away from it initially because it means putting all my stuff out there – and some of it ain't pretty. But as I said, I know I am not the only one whose life is not picture-perfect. In fact, what I know now is that *no one's* life is perfect, some people are just better at hiding the ugly stuff. But it's like papering over the cracks in a house that's falling apart: you have to fix the foundation, eradicate the damp and the mould, and deal with all the stuff that's festering in the dark before you can fill in the cracks and put up that beautiful wallpaper.

I finally made the decision in September 2023, when I went to the Woman Evolve Conference in Arlington, Texas. On the first night, Pastor Sarah Jakes preached, and I wept. I don't remember exactly what she said, but I knew that God was telling me to stop running away – to write my book. I felt almost like Jonah, who ended up somewhere he wasn't supposed to be because he was avoiding sharing God's message.

Back at my hotel, I wrote down tons of notes and finally said to myself, 'Yes, I will do it.' I know it was God who had spoken to me because as soon as I called my then potential publisher, whom I had previously put off, she jumped with excitement and immediately got the ball rolling. No complications, nothing: simply a book God wanted to be brought out. In that same month, the dots connected about what had happened to me as a child, the sexual violation I had experienced. We will get into that later.

Just then, I realised I had a responsibility to liberate other girls and women who might be living their lives burdened by something that is not their fault.

On the path I travelled I have learnt – first through my studying and then through the twists and turns my career took – that my calling in life is to be a healer. I don't mean it in the traditional sense of a doctor, a psychologist or even a healer who anoints you with oil while praying for you. No, I heal through stories. My vulnerability is my stethoscope. My podcast and YouTube channel are my doctor's room, and there I make use of my expertise – my life experiences, my pain and my sense of shame. I don't put myself out there because I enjoy it. I share because I want to give others permission to look at their lives and identify patterns, emotions and behaviour that up to now they have accepted as being just part of life. I share because I want others to start letting their emotions flow. I share because when women heal, generations heal. I share because I have watched too many women in my life suffer from lifestyle diseases because they choose to be strong. I share in order to normalise talking about those shameful, hurtful things we keep hidden. I share because so many of us, I realised, are never taught how to process all that we feel.

I share because so many of us, too, grew up in homes where verbal and physical abuse was the norm, where name-calling and bullying were seen as funny and we were made to think there was something wrong with us if we didn't get the joke. We are still hurting; we're triggered every time we hear those jokes again, even as adults.

I share because girls are taught that being a woman means taking the knife by the sharp end and boys believe being a man means never crying or showing emotion.

I was 24 when I understood that not talking about stuff is holding us back, and hurting our communities. This book is my way of showing that talking, sharing and processing are necessary, if only for our own sake.

We need to be allowed to feel, to be angry, to make mistakes and, ultimately, to heal.

I first got an inkling of this with my newsletter, 'Sunday Nuggets'. My goal being to connect more with our Wisdom & Wellness community, in the newsletter I share my thoughts on personal topics such as forgiveness and mother wounds, along with some lessons. What I presumed was mainly for marketing purposes turned out to be a challenge from God, and if I had known how personal and emotional the newsletter would become I might have bowed out. But it continues to this day, and every Sunday I get messages from people about how deeply they relate, how they have been freed and that they will try again.

I might be a tad dramatic. Okay, I admit it, there's no 'might' about it. I *am* dramatic; I know this about myself and I accept it. Being the drama queen that I am, in the lead-up to turning 30, I felt I had to get my life in order. To be honest, and upon intense reflection, I am now a few steps ahead of where I thought I would be. But as you'll discover, I believe in continuous growth. Two major things stood out for me as I stared 30 in the face: firstly, I had built walls around myself in fear of judgement. I realised that I can't show up as perfectly as I imagine everybody wants me to. (I also don't know who this 'everybody' is, but yeah.) And secondly, I lacked the ability to speak up when things made me uncomfortable. I hated, I mean really *hated*, confrontation (even more than my crooked teeth, which I spent a lot of money fixing).

So I made a decision: I would start addressing the elephant in the room in real time.

With my husband.

With my work team.

With my friends.

With my family.

With everyone.

That has led to a bunch of blow-ups, but it has also helped me identify just who my people are.

I feel like I may be scaring you off before we've even begun. Relax! I am not playing hopscotch on people's heads and telling them where to get off. It's actually quite the opposite: it entails a whole lot of breathing in and out, and politely sharing how something makes me feel, instead of waiting until I can no longer look the person in the eye and am ready to explode.

I learnt this the hard way.

My relationship – very serious and consistent relationship – with the gym started in 2019. The first few sessions were a living hell, with my DD breasts popping up in my face with every burpee, but after a few months I finally got into it. It was just my trainer and I until we were joined by Bonolo, whose beauty and fitness blew my mind. I couldn't help but start a conversation with her. That conversation led to a friendship, a working relationship and a sisterhood that would change my life.

Brenden and I were new parents in desperate need of a date night. Bonolo worked part-time as an au pair, and I found the courage to ask her to help us out. She was so great with Nuri that it became a frequent thing, and soon she was assisting in my life too. She shifted from being an au pair to a friend to an informal personal assistant and, eventually, to being the manager at my salon.

Bonolo is very smart and organised, not to mention reliable, so everything was going well.

'Mpoomy, I am pregnant.'

That evening my kitchen was filled with joy, as I knew how much Bonolo wanted to be a mother. We were so happy. This was her rainbow and miracle baby, and that was all that mattered. We didn't anticipate the toll her morning sickness – the intense nausea and vomiting that is hyperemesis gravidarum – would take on her body. The extended time she had to take off affected my business and finances. As a friend, I knew I had to show up for her; as an employer – and a sleep-deprived mother of two toddlers – I could not allow this to continue.

I had two choices: let Bonolo go or grudgingly accept the increasing tension. I could no longer afford to keep her and the salon. I could also no longer show up as a friend because of the heightened resentment between us.

Who fires a pregnant woman, you may ask? A 26-year-old who fears confrontation and is trying to build a business and …

Instead of having an honest conversation as a leader and a friend, I chose the easy way out. I lived with the guilt of what had happened, but we remained friends. Even in those first days of my meeting her baby, Kabo, the tension was so thick a knife could slice through it, but love filled the room.

Things began to improve: Bonolo was on the hunt for a new job, and my personal brand was starting to thrive. Nobody, to this day, can organise my life like she did. So we started working together again. And this is where the big lesson happened, in a tough conversation filled with tears; I had to face the pain I had put her through.

It's never easy to hear how you hurt someone, especially when it was not your intention. But you learn to sit in the discomfort and take accountability. I am convinced an honest relationship really began that day; we gave conflict space and we could look each other in the eye and apologise.

Truth be told, working together the second time around was also not a success. As someone still learning to deal with confrontation, learning to be a leader, the situation became too much for me to handle. Our working relationship ended. But we gave each other invaluable lessons, and she is now a sister. She still organises my children's birthday parties, and planned my 30th. We have seen the worst and best of each other. We know things that nobody should ever know, and I would choose her over and over again.

I have since learnt that the people who are meant to be in your life will stay even if there is a disagreement, as long as it is dealt with in an open and healthy manner. Conflict is an opportunity to learn and realign with each other.

So, yes, I talk about some uncomfortable stuff in this book. But don't worry, it was discussed with the relevant people before I put pen to paper. And if it hasn't been discussed, that's because the person concerned is no longer in my life – with good reason. As writer Anne Lamott points out, we own everything that's ever happened to us, it belongs to us, and if people don't want us to speak about it, well, fam, they should've treated us better!

REFLECTION

Dear reader, you are going to discover a reflection at the end of each chapter. I urge you to take this journey with me to reflect on your own experiences in the hope of finding the spots in your life where you are tender. I am not a psychologist, but I've spent a lot of time in therapy and one of the things my therapist has always recommended is journalling.

This is your chance to write down your thoughts. Some of them might be painful, some might be joyful. They are for your eyes only. You don't need to censor yourself – put everything down. Hopefully, you will find healing in the writing. Yes, I'm giving you permission to write in this book. I write in my book, so you can do the same. And if a friend wants to borrow it, gift them their own copy!

Let's jump in ...

Think of an experience you had that involved conflict. Maybe the person didn't mean to hurt you, but they've done something – without even realising it – to upset you. No one likes dealing with confrontation, but you may need to do something about it before things get out of hand.

Ask yourself:
- How do I handle confrontation?
- Do I deal with an issue when it arises?
- Or do I let the issue fester and then explode?

Tips for handling confrontation:
- Always be polite.
- Use 'I' when confronting someone. For example, *I feel disrespected when you speak to me like that.*
- Deal with issues as soon as they come up.
- Write it all down.

2

Birthday cake

There is an old saying that goes something like this: 'To know where you're going, you need to know where you come from.' For me to be able to move on from childhood hurts and confusion, I had to go back and see what my parents' lives had been like when they were growing up, what had moulded them – good and bad – into the people they are today. Once I opened myself to that process, so many things that seemed incomprehensible started to make sense.

My mother grew up in a strict household. If her home was not clean and her children's school marks were average or below, my grandmother would stand on their hands in her high heels or throw a wet dishcloth at them. It could be seen as abuse by today's standards, but at that time it was not out of the ordinary; she was just considered strict.

My grandfather, Sam (or Khuyu, as we called him since we were toddlers), was a respected teacher and head of department, and my grandmother, Agnes, was the principal at one of the best-run schools in the township in Middelburg. Naturally, my mother studied teaching. I don't think it was one of those purpose- and passion-driven career choices we have now. It was a good option for a black woman when – during apartheid – not many options were available for them. Luckily for my mom, teaching was not just a job, it is her calling.

She started teaching at the age of about 22 at a high school – Ekwazini Secondary – Mhluzi, a township in Middelburg where we lived. The school started off well, but then things got really bad, from kids failing to smoking and taking drugs to behaving in all sorts of unruly ways. She would take me with her to school during my exam time or when I had a day off, and I couldn't even use the kids' bathroom because of its terrible condition, not to mention the danger of being in there alone. It was giving *Yizo Yizo* vibes, great in a TV show, not so great in real life.

But my mom loved the children. To this day we meet people who greet her with 'Ma'am, do you still remember me?' And I am shocked every time, not only because she does remember them but because they look twice her age – testimony to the harshness of their lives. I have often wanted to blurt out, 'But, Mom, is that not the parent?' and have bitten my tongue just in time.

My mother met most of her lifelong friends and best friends there. She would walk out the house smelling like Far Away perfume and wearing her mid-length leather jacket that she LOVED. Because it was from America, it was padded for their harsh winters so it was good quality and a daily for her. It's probably back in style now, and she could still rock it, but my mom gives everything away, so it's long gone.

In those days she had long, dark hair that she kept in a low ponytail, showing off her beautiful forehead. Every six weeks she would go to the salon to have her hair relaxed, something she always made room for in her limited budget. Coming home with a headache or even a migraine was the norm for her, and she would nap in the afternoons while I played at the neighbour's. Now that I am older and we talk openly, it's clear to me how stressful her life was, trying to make ends meet and raising three young children with only part-time help, not to mention coping with the issues that accompanied nurturing a blended family. With all that and those tight ponytails, it's no wonder her head suffered.

My mother is happier now, in her 50s, than she was back then.

'On my first day of school, I knew I had to get a job. I was about seven.'

He didn't have a uniform. That's why my dad didn't finish school. I was under the impression that my dad left school because he didn't like it, or it was too far to walk, but I was wrong. My dad didn't know how poor they were until his first day of school when he had to borrow a school uniform to register and then return it to the owner after. Because the teachers loved him, they helped him with a uniform, but the scar of poverty had made its mark and it was too deep. He immediately shifted his focus from being a boy to getting a job to feed his family, and so he spent most of his primary school days looking for jobs as a gardener.

It was not until he was 11 years old that he officially called it quits. He got a job working for farm owners in the area, as a playmate for their son Andrew. My grandmother did not want him to leave school, but as far as he was concerned he was making money and there was no point in continuing. The plan was to be a gardener for Andrew's family, but the only 'job' available was to be Andrew's minder and playmate – kind of like an au pair.

'Andrew was two. His second birthday party was the first time I saw a birthday cake. I had never celebrated a birthday, let alone been given a cake.' So began a lifelong friendship with Andrew and my dad's first real chance of escaping poverty.

Poverty strips people of their dignity, and they have to fight to make it out. My dad is a fighter, a gentle fighter. His smile is from the soul, as he directs all of his anger and pain onto poverty. He fought his way out, and not only has he made sure we didn't know what poverty felt like, he and my mom have given us a foundation that can only lead to generational wealth. My shoes have never had holes. I have never not known whether there will be food to eat, even if it meant my mom had to wake up at 4 am to knead dough to make vetkoek. I thought she was preparing a special lunch, but she was mixing the only ingredients we had at home so we never went a day hungry.

I've received a few of those 'School fees not paid' letters, but so did many of my black classmates. We probably thought, 'Oh well, it's letters for the black kids.' But I and my siblings were fine. We had the clothes and equipment to participate in sports, we always had lunch, and we got new clothes every Christmas holiday and just before the winter holidays.

My parents met at a house party in KwaZulu-Natal through a mutual friend. My mom was studying at the University of Zululand and my dad was visiting the friend, who was at university with her. They hit it off. But then my dad returned to Ermelo for work and my mom heard nothing more from him. It's his story to tell, but I think the encounter may have been a fling to him. Not to my mom; she was promised heaven and earth and so she went searching for him. She called up their mutual friend, Uncle Fire (as we affectionately knew him), asking him to tell my dad to get it together. Uncle Fire clearly did a great job because, 30 years later, it's still my parents I dash home to cuddle with every time I'm having a bad day.

I was too young to know my dad as a truck driver. I did know him as a truck owner, though, and his truck always broke down. When my husband considered investing in a truck, my dad was the first to tell him about all the breakdowns he should expect. My dad is an optimist of note, so you must know how bad it was. (PS: We didn't buy a truck.)

My dad used to work for a company called Camden, and as one of their truck drivers he travelled all over South Africa. I asked him once if he had ever been to Cape Town. At his yes, the questions tumbled out of my mouth:

'Did you fly there? Did you go to the beach? How was the weather?' Only for him to casually relate that he had delivered carrots, in the middle of the night.

I was probably around two, and my mother was on leave, so my parents thought it was a good idea for us to tag along on one of my dad's deliveries, and it happened to be in KZN, a six-hour drive from Middelburg by car. Because it was a carrot delivery, I spent most of the trip feasting on carrots – so much that my mother never misses a chance to share my carrot indulgence story. I owe my eyesight to that carrot truck trip. If we are being honest, I can barely handle a two-hour road trip in our comfortable car with air-con, a sound system and *Bluey* as entertainment for my kids. Imagine doing that in a truck? With a two-year-old? So next time you see a massive truck parked in the middle of the night to rest, just keep in mind I was once in one of them with my mom and dad, drowning in carrots.

'Ubab'm uzoku killa dead!'

This was enough to put any adult in their place. Whether they were trying to invade my space or discipline me, letting them know that my dad would kill them was my way of reminding them who was boss. I was a daddy's girl, and everybody had to know it.

My dad is a softie, a loving and present father, but he is human. When we start seeing our parents as humans, we are more forgiving. I remember the first time he broke my heart.

While trying out to be on the chess team, I had to remain after school. My dad fetched me early. Despite my explaining that I needed to stay to make it to the next round, he insisted he had a meeting to get to. I understood that; what upset me was getting home and watching him simply lie down on the couch. I lost out on trying for something I could've been good at, and I was lied to by the man I loved the most.

My mother remembers being equally upset and thought maybe he didn't realise how important extramurals are for a child. I suspect there was something more serious going on; perhaps he was faced with debt or disappointment or something painful. He took a nap when we got home, though he was never one to sleep during the day; nor was he unsupportive of our activities. I was a child who saw only opportunities, and as far as I was concerned, my father was denying me an opportunity. If he had explained it more clearly to me then, I might've understood, but while growing up, if our parents said no, that was it, we knew better than to argue. (I still don't know how to play chess, having forgotten everything I learnt then.)

With my own children, I am often tempted to say, simply, 'Because I said so.' But experiences like this one with my dad make me swallow those words and take the time to explain to my children why they can't do something. If they are unhappy about it, they are allowed to express that.

In asking my dad about little Godfrey, I was able to reconcile my heartbreak. And although I didn't get as many birthday gifts as I would have loved to, all *my* birthdays had a birthday cake.

REFLECTION

Not all of us are lucky enough to still have our parents around. But if they are, it can be very helpful to ask them what their upbringing was like, or, if they're not around, to speak to people who knew them. Only then do we get a clearer picture of what made them the way they are.

- Think back to your childhood, to any time your mother or father or caregiver disappointed you in some way. Did you ever take time to process your disappointment?
- If they are around, and you feel comfortable doing so, ask them if they remember the incident and why they behaved the way they did.

  You might be surprised to find out that something was happening in their own lives that led to them to behave that way. Perhaps their parents were not around, or didn't set the best example for them when they were growing up.

  This is not to give them a free pass but to understand why they did what they did and who they were or needed to be to survive their circumstances.

  Once we understand something, and can make peace with it, it's much easier to let it go.
- Write it all down.

3

Not planned
but loved

When I came along, in 1994, my mother was 22 and had just
started teaching, and my dad was driving trucks across the country
for days at a time. Without trying or planning to have a baby, my
mom was suddenly queasy, and it didn't take long for the two lines
on the pregnancy test stick to confirm her suspicions. Although
my parents were not yet married, marriage was frequently discussed. It was only a matter of time and money before my dad
would honour his first words to my mom: 'I'm going make you
my wife.'

My parents decided to hide me from their families, until
ilobola – the bride price – was paid. They were not ashamed, but
if the cost of inhlawulo could be spared for a few months of a
privately kept pregnancy, it was worth it. Inhlawulo is the dam-
ages paid to the family of a woman who becomes pregnant out
of wedlock by the father of the future child. My father quickly
paid lobola to show the intention of marrying my mother. In my
mother's words, they 'cheated her parents' and kept quiet about

her pregnancy. Not even my grandmother knew. By the time the news came out, they were husband and wife, at least traditionally.

The lobola negotiations were full of drama, because of my mother's uncle, who prided himself on being the difficult relative who threw his weight around. As the chief negotiator, it was his responsibility to oversee the process, a role he relished. Everyone needed to understand that he was in control, and nothing could happen without him. For those who may not know, ilobola is an opportunity for the families to get to know each other and build relations, so some playful conflict is encouraged. The key word here is 'playful', but Uncle Peter took it a little too far. To this day my father's family roars with laughter and horror when they speak of the chaos he almost created. But things worked out in the end and the day was successful. My grandfather did insist on walking cows, which later explained why my dad was adamant about my lobola proceedings too.

Thinking about it now, I wonder why there was a rush. My mother's parents both had children out of wedlock, and my father's parents never married, even after 11 children (imagine your pelvic floor after that!). My grandmother remained MaNdlovu while my grandfather, who we just recently found out is not actually my grandfather, continued to work away from home eCinci in KwaZulu-Natal. That is a story for another book.

The first few years of my life took place at my grandmother's house. My baby pictures show a pretty soft life. My grandparents were the first black people to build a house in a white suburb in Middelburg, called Aerorand, and aunt Boocy was the first black girl at the school – Middelburg Primary – I then attended. Boocy is tough, very strong and quick to defend, but she is also very sweet, and you can't help but like her. According to my grandmother, she had no trouble being the only black child in a white school. She was treated quite fairly, and and she befriended the white girls but I wonder how easy it actually was for her. She must've encountered some of what Trevor Noah refers to as that premium South African racism. I think being in that environment probably toughened her up.

In one of my favourite photos taken at my grandmother's house, I am seated at the kitchen island blowing out a candle on my birthday cake. The kitchen island is enough to show you the kind of grandparents I have. For a black family to have something like that was *huge*, and it was one of the first things I wanted to build in my dream house: a great big beautiful kitchen island. My birthday cake was round and vanilla-flavoured, with fluffy white icing, pink and white candles, and two cherries on top. To this day a plain vanilla cake with white icing is my absolute favourite. You would never catch me ordering a chocolate cake on any day!

In the photo my hair is short, although I had lost the chubby cheeks and my bow legs. I still had skinny arms which was obvious thanks to how my faded green two-piece snuggled my arms. My mother always kept my hair natural but softened it with Hair Glo – a semi-relaxer we grew up on that made our hair more manageable. We eventually transitioned to something stronger, Dark and Lovely, to try to get the silky look shown on the pink box. It never happened; my hair always broke, and we would start over with the Afro. Now, of course, it's a popular choice to have natural hair, but growing up, we all wanted to be Becky with the 'good' hair. The softer the texture, the 'luckier' you were.

3935 Melato Street, Mhluzi Ext 1, is where all my first vivid memories began. Our little shoebox-shaped, flat-roofed home was a typical four-room house in the township. The bedroom was right next to the TV room, I mean you stepped out of the room and you were with everyone in the TV room, and right next to the bedroom we shared as kids was our parents' room, and with just one step you were right by the bathroom we all shared next to the kitchen. We might have had the smallest house in the street, but it was always spotless. Sundays featured the smell of chicken stew on a plate with beetroot and coleslaw, accompanied by the voices of Whitney Houston and Puff Johnson, followed by a nap on our maroon couches. The garden was filled with magnificent hydrangeas and lush green grass that my dad dedicated his afternoons to manicuring. That is the thing with my parents: they have always had a way of bringing out the beauty in everything.

The best part of my childhood was lived in that house.

Although I attended a Model C school in town, where we would later move, I spent most of my time playing in the street. We would play house, hopscotch and skipping rope until the Apollo lights came on and we'd get in trouble day after day for 'missing curfew'. Sometimes my mother was so angry she would make me pick out my own tree branch for my hiding. I would go for the smallest, thinnest one, but even so those suckers would sting like hell.

I was always the youngest among my friends; my best friend Nonkululeko lived two houses down and made it her personal mission to protect me from the big kids. I never really fitted in. The way I spoke was different, the way my parents did things was different. My father was pretty much raised by a white family (Andrew's family), so he brought many of their principles into our home. I might have been unsure about a lot of things, but one thing I knew was that I was being raised to be responsible and successful – to be a leader. I don't know if all my other siblings felt this way, but I certainly did.

I don't remember being introduced to my older siblings, but I do recall how much I loved and admired them. I wanted to be just like Tunky. Six years older, she had a beautiful chubby-cheeked face and long legs that turned heads everywhere she went; she wore her hair in a Toni Braxton cut and, boy, did I want one. Tough Guy made me laugh; no one could match him when it came to humour. From morning till night I followed him around; he pretended to hate it, but deep down he knew I was a pretty cool little sister. He was well known and popular.

My siblings didn't live with us but came home every holiday. Then all my friends from our street would flock to our home to see Tough Guy. I literally counted the days to their arrival and loved every minute of having them around. We would hire cassettes from Mr Video (remember those?), each of us choosing one. We would go to sleep late at night, or exchange stories and giggle until the sun rose. Because all of us slept in that one tiny room, we struggled to keep it clean, at least according to my mother's standards. Tough Guy's black boots filling the room remains a standing joke. I can still smell them!

Thirteen days before I turned four, Nonto was born. The previous day, my dad and I took a road trip to Johannesburg to visit one of my uncles. I don't have the full context of why this happened, but I have been married long enough to know that pregnancy hormones and dynamics have a way of pushing a marriage to its limits. According to my dad, my mom was a bit on the Godzilla side during her pregnancy with Nonto and, you know what, as a mom of two, I get it.

There's a picture in my head that sums up all my feelings towards my little sister as a child.

It was a winter morning in our house eMhluzi; we were getting ready to go somewhere important. I picked out my favourite olive-green velvet two-piece, and a bandana that had brunette Caucasian hair hanging from it. I was excited about my outfit, *so* excited, and along came Nonto dressed in exactly the same clothes. In the picture we are sitting on the kitchen counter, with my head nearly hitting the ceiling. (An indication of the size of the house, not my height.) I was sad, I was angry; as an adult I can finally say I had no room, then, to be an individual. And I needed to be.

My mother forced us to wear the same outfits and do the same things; I had to share everything I had with my sister, including my friends. From being my mother's only child to having to share her with this baby, whom I also had to look out for, was too much for my four- to five-year-old brain. Now, I realise that I sensed a large part of my identity being stripped away, which led to intense resentment. Our relationship would be complicated until I was about 16. As siblings we loved each other, but we also despised each other. Or rather, she learnt to dislike me because of the way I treated her.

Fearful of my mom's reaction, I didn't criticise her out loud, but I did other things. I now regret it, but I pictured her being wiped from the face of the earth. I gave her the silent treatment. I would come home from school, prepare food for myself and tell her to do it for herself, knowing that she was too young. One afternoon I made popcorn, and when Nonto asked for some I gave her three kernels. My mom was not impressed.

On consideration, it wasn't so much that I found her irritating. She was such an introverted child, minding her own business and never asking for anything. It was how she took all of my mother's attention. I was unprepared, I believe, for what it meant to have a younger sibling; after four years of being the centre of attention, it felt like rejection. There it is: the presence of my sister felt like a rejection of me. It also did not help that her arrival meant there was someone I could compare myself to. I was so busy and active, I got in trouble quite a lot. A part of me felt like I should be more like her to avoid trouble. But I wasn't her, and I couldn't be her.

My daughter is a clear reflection of me. Nuri gives me the beautiful opportunity to experience myself as a child, without labels. She needs her individuality, space and creativity like she needs breath. Everything she does, she takes personally and seriously. If it's not from the heart, she does not do it. When she doesn't feel heard, she will say, 'But, Mama, I like it.'

From when she was very young, we were not allowed to choose Nuri's outfits. She was set on a tutu, which she called a 'ballerina', and a top. When I would force her to wear a tracksuit, her heart would break into a million pieces. Her head would drop, her shoulders would slump; she would start to cry. Not a tantrum, but sobs that would grow louder and louder.

'You are not being kind, Mommy.'

And: 'But I *like* ballerinas.'

The tracksuit was a denial of her individuality and she wasn't having it.

Most three-year-olds do this, but I get how she feels. I recognise the feeling so vividly, and I hate to see her experience it.

This is why Brenden and I employ gentle and conscious parenting, something our parents did not do. *When we know better, we do better.* They didn't know any better. Every time I picked out an outfit and my mother made Nonto look exactly like me was an instance in which I sensed the need to fight for my life, fight to be seen. Fight to be Mpumi, not Mpumi-and-Nonto.

Nonto and I shared many incredible moments of playing and enjoying our childhood together. She never stole my clothes, or messed up my things to aggravate me. The only sin she ever committed towards me was making me feel like I had to work hard to be seen and to be approved of, like her. And work hard I did. I became an overachiever of note.

Isn't it crazy how we build up so much dislike, irritation and hurt around someone, and it has nothing to do with them but rather everything to do with us? Homing in on our childhood, I see how my battle to be seen and acknowledged was projected onto my little sister. I lost out on years of a friendship I could've had as a little girl. I robbed her of a big sister she could talk to about her first crush or her first kiss or her first period. At 30 and 26 we are starting to catch up on those things.

She never retaliated against my emotional outbursts towards her. I recall only one occasion when things got physical.

I was responsible for cleaning the kitchen and living room, Nonto the bathrooms and passages. In true Nonto style, it would be in her own time, which was mostly the middle of the day. My best friend was visiting and we were rushing off.

'The floor is wet.'

'So? I want to pass.'

'Don't you dare pass!'

The argument escalated into a physical fight, ended by my best friend. Nobody was seriously hurt, but like the floor our outfits were soaked.

Physical fights never sting as much as the emotional ones do. Nevertheless, as I said, it was rare for Nonto to fight back. She went inward. You have to earn her trust, no matter who you are. I like that about her, but a part of me feels sad too. As the middle child, whom we always assumed was okay, she had to learn to take care of herself by digging an emotional shelter deep within.

We have begun the tough process of mining it. I blamed myself for being so mean to Nonto, preventing her from being heard. But she does not remember our childhood the way that I do, and has never seen me as the sister who hated her.

I am glad I went to therapy, glad I started dealing with me. In forgiving little Mpumi for this, I have given myself the opportunity to get to know Nonto without feeling unseen. And what an incredible and funny girl she is. The minute I hop onto TikTok, every second video seems to relate to the pair of us. I have a very strange sense of humour; not even my husband understands it as she does. Nonto and I will roll on the floor, laughing at the same joke over and over. She might just be the only person who really gets my humour, and I hers.

I was six when Mtho, now Uncle Jack, was born. There's a picture of my mother holding him and you would think she had stolen him. My mother has beautiful dark skin and, at that time, he was practically white. Not light-skinned, white.

Parents always say, 'We love you all equally.' You and I know that isn't true. In our family we knew who the favourite was; I hate to break it to you, fam, but it wasn't me.

My mother's world was complete. That little boy had her wrapped around his finger, especially because he was fragile and had bad eczema. My son has eczema too; I found out it's genetic. I have it under control for the most part, but there are random breakouts that get me in my feels. It doesn't come close to what my brother experienced while he was growing up, though: he was allergic to every single thing you could imagine. Because he was so pale, his face would flush from breakouts, and in the folds of his knees, arms and neck his skin was as dry as a crocodile. He loved bananas and citrus fruit, but the minute he touched them the guitar playing would start. That's what Tough Guy called his scratching – guitar playing – because of the way he would 'strum' his whole body trying to get rid of the itching.

Despite the little my parents earned, my mom had to cater to Uncle Jack's diet, test out a million creams from multiple derma-tologists and buy him top-quality clothing. Come to think of it, maybe that's why I wanted to be a dermatologist. I've never really connected the two things until now, but of course, I wanted to help my brother.

He was the golden egg of the family; he softened the home; he was sickly, but also active and cute as hell. Why I wasn't jealous of him the way I was jealous of my sister, I don't know. He came just two years after her. One thing was clear, though, by the time he arrived: I knew that being a baby was no longer an option; I had to start being responsible. Nobody gave me that responsibility. I felt it.

REFLECTION

No one can wind us up like our siblings, am I right? Perhaps I would've wished my sister away when we were growing up. Now I can't do without her.

Think of your own sisters and brothers ...
- What are your relationships with your siblings like?
- Are there issues from your childhood that you haven't dealt with?
- Were you bullied by a sibling?
- Perhaps you were the bully?
- Did you sense that one of the siblings was the favourite? How did that make you feel?

- Or were you the favourite? How did it make your siblings feel?
- What would you like to say to your siblings now?
- Write it all down.

4

Feel the pain

We all have scars. Some are from childhood mishaps, others are marks left on both our bodies and our minds, and some are from experiences that hurt us emotionally.

Nonkululeko, my childhood bestie, was two years older than me. Our afternoons were filled with adventure. We would scramble eggs for lunch, grab some apples and play together until my mother called me home. Because Nonkululeko's parents were older and more easygoing than mine, we preferred playing at her house. It was painted bright pink – you read that right! – and we loved it. During the cold months I was allowed to stay a little later, the entire house being made warm and cosy by the family's old coal stove. (Winter has been my favourite season ever since.) The coal was kept outside in a huge wooden box built by her dad in such a way that a steep ladder was needed to reach it. The box soon became our make-believe house.

My mother warned me against climbing the ladder, and she was right.

'Nonkululeko, follow me, I'm going upstairs.'

Clack, clack, clack …

As I reached the highest point, I missed a step and fell. While drifting in and out of sleep to the sound of John from *Days of Our Lives*, my head was pounding, and my mother was furious. This memory is pretty vivid because I never made it home in time for *Days of Our Lives*, just *The Bold and the Beautiful*.

Thinking about my Grade R year at Dennisig Primary fills me with tension. Our class was mostly black kids because we were the English class, so we only mingled with the others during break time and to be honest I can't even remember speaking to the white kids besides Chantel, who was the only white kid in our class. She didn't speak Afrikaans and her parents were teachers in the school. I was a petite child and a bit of a goody two-shoes. The other children were bigger than me and a little rowdy. I did not feel part of the cool crowd unless I rebelled. I never felt safe there, and now I realise that it was because I was bullied. I had friends, but I knew that I couldn't show fear; I had to act tough to survive.

The school lawn was immaculate, lush and green; it looked untouched. One early afternoon, the bell rang loudly.

Tring, tring, tring …

I can still hear it.

On my way back to class – in my denim shorts, red school T-shirt and big Afro, with not a care in the world – I raced to cross the lawn. But I didn't make it. One moment I could hear the voices and footsteps of the other kids around me, the next moment I woke up to dead silence and my face caught in the fine-wired fence that protected the lawn.

My six-year-old brain fought hard to shield me from that day – many of the details remain elusive even now. All I remember is that I opened my eyes to the greenest grass I had ever seen, and I was totally alone. Leaving skin behind on that fence, I walked myself to the sickroom.

I have a theory that white people see black people as tough soldiers, that our skin and bodies can handle anything – we are somehow created to withstand harsh conditions. Perhaps that's why I was not taken to casualty, nor was my mother called to come to fetch me. The wounds were cleaned as though the damage was no worse than a small graze on my knee. Had a white child been injured in this way, the situation would most likely have been treated as the emergency it was. I'd seen the care the teachers showed the other learners – from hair pulling to nosebleeds, they were looked after.

But I was not seen.

Our school transport picked us up as usual, and my mother was waiting for me outside our unfenced yard. The tears in her eyes, her expression full of confusion, anger and fear, confirmed the seriousness of the damage. I could have lost an eye; the scar that runs by my right eye is proof that God's gentle hand saved me.

Every now and then, I wonder how I digested the trauma of the moment.

The grass was left untouched, and my face was changed forever.

In the years that followed, my mother rubbed tissue oil on my scars. At first it hurt, then it became a tedious and redundant exercise. The oil made my scars more visible, but my mother persevered, and over time they faded and then became a part of my face.

The emotional scars still visit me. This is probably at least partly why pain and hurt have not always been significant factors for me. I became so good at downplaying pain that I created a standing joke: I would rather be fetched by an ambulance than quit. I think it's six-year-old Mpumi reminding me of that day when, even with deep cuts and blood all over my face, life continued as normal. Nobody stopped for me, nobody asked questions. Nobody cared enough to realise the damage that had been done to my skin. It was just another day at school.

During both my pregnancies, I did not consider taking maternity leave but worked until my babies were ready to pop out. A few days after giving birth, my laptop was open. The day after I almost lost my life in a car accident, I still had responsibilities to meet. Life had to go on.

In a televised conversation with Oprah and Tyler Perry, trauma therapist and life coach Dr Anita Phillips speaks about resilience, reminding us that resilience starts with admitting the pain and not downplaying it. If a glass is hit with an axe, it will shatter; if a wooden chair is hit with an axe, it will not shatter but it will be damaged. If a glass is put in a bowl of water, it will float, but a wooden chair will rot. In other words, different conditions and environments hurt different people differently. But whatever the circumstances, no hurt is too small. That's something I've needed to learn.

I have downplayed some of the biggest traumas in my life by comparing them to how blessed I have been and how others have had life worse. I believe in gratitude but I am no soldier. I need to stop treating myself as one, and my advice is that you should too.

REFLECTION

There are still times when I want to get something done, so I push through even though I'm exhausted or not feeling great. What can I say? I'm a work in progress. Also, let's be honest, sometimes there is a deadline and you don't want to let people down. The trick is knowing when you really must push through and when the earth is not going to stop turning if you don't attend a meeting. Sometimes we are very bad at seeing the difference.

- Think about the times you minimised your own pain.
- How could you have handled the situation differently?
- Give that child, or young woman or mother, a hug and tell her it's okay to feel pain, it's okay to take time off.
- Now start putting it into practice. If you're sick, stay in bed and get better. If you have flu, or a migraine or bad period cramps, speak up! People are not mind readers. Also, gal pal, you know if men had cramps they would get a full week off, with Schedule 6 painkillers, so don't feel bad that you need to take one day for yourself.
- Write it all down.

In case you need someone to say it out loud, the world will keep turning as long as God wills it. Rest!

How Did We Get Here?

5

Silver threads

Parents who were often tough on their children tend to relax and spoil their grandchildren. From the stories my parents have told me, I know that this is certainly the case for us.

During our time in Mhluzi, I used to love visiting my maternal grandmother, who lived in the suburbs. My Gogo, she was the coolest grandmother, in her maroon Mazda that was always spotless and you were guaranteed to find some sweets in it. That's where I got my sweet tooth. As a school principal, she was well known for changing the lives of her students, many of whom achieved astoundingly high marks. Her spacious office had a wide window that allowed her to see the whole school, and on some occasions she would take me there with her. I felt special walking through those corridors – I was the principal's smart and pretty granddaughter.

My grandmother would pick me up for sleepovers and weekends spent together in her beautiful home, which felt like heaven on earth. She would wake me up each morning with a cup of tea, and serve oats paired with yoghurt and fruit on a tray while

I reclined on her white leather couches, which nobody else was allowed to lounge on. We would go all over town running errands, during which she would spoil me with a little shopping, but the best memory was buying a packet of 100 Fruit Chews and finishing them together in the car.

'Just one more, Gogo …'

Before we knew it, the packet was empty.

Life got complicated when Boocy had my cousin Amy at 17. I watched a soft and loving grandmother slowly switch back into mother mode in her late 50s as Boocy went back to school. She had to adapt to changing nappies, paying school fees and helping with homework, and I realised with a sense of sadness that our connection got lost in those moments. I was no longer the focus of her attention. Grandmothers raising children is often unavoidable in our society, but I don't think they are meant to do this – it robs them of the joy of easing up and playing good cop.

Once or twice a year, my paternal grandmother, MaNdlovu, would reluctantly leave her home, emakhaya, to visit us. Though she loved us, she hated the six-hour journey. Our nights together were filled with giggles and bedtime stories, inganekwane, as we surrounded her in our tiny bedroom. We didn't see her as often as we'd have liked. Whenever we visited there, I had fun with my many cousins but had few intimate moments with her. When she visited us, I felt like I got to know her a little better. With age my hair is becoming more and more like hers: full-bodied and grey. I feel connected to her by those silver threads.

I am in awe of how well both my grandmothers did.

Gogo pretty much raised herself and her siblings. Her mother departed to marry another man, leaving the children to fend for themselves. When puberty hit, my grandmother had no choice but to make her own bra using a maize meal sack. (She has tried to explain how she did this, but I still struggle to connect the dots.)

I don't think love was a feature while growing up: survival was the most important thing. However, Gogo is a smart woman who, through her resilient spirit, did pretty well for herself. When Gogo met Sam, my grandfather, a tall, dark, handsome and intelligent man, they set out to get her educated. Using the materials my teacher grandfather would bring home from school, Gogo studied by candlelight. While raising children and building a home, she qualified with distinction, becoming a teacher and eventually a principal.

We did not have a chance to find out all MaNdlovu's stories, but I know that she was raised by her sister in Swaziland, never met her parents and somehow ended up in KZN. Despite never learning to write or read, she knew the Bible better than anyone I know, having learnt it from my cousin reading it to her.

Psalm 23 was her favourite scripture. Without skipping a word, she would pray it over us in beautiful, pure isiZulu.

'The Lord is my shepherd, I shall not want.'

MaNdlovu raised my dad and his 11 siblings by herself, while my grandfather would go for months at a time looking for work to provide for the family. I don't know how she managed it. Her mornings began at 4 am in prayer and sweeping her yard; she kept active all day, and her home was always filled with strangers that she took in. Her silver threads carried a wisdom only God can give, and she passed them on to me.

'Nobelungu' was her name for me when she saw something in me that she couldn't articulate.

We are our ancestors' wildest dreams, right?

REFLECTION

Not all of us are privileged to have known our grandparents or to still have them around. But maybe you've heard stories about them from your parents, or there is a figure in your life who is like a granny or grandpa to you.

- Did you know your grandparents? Or do you have someone in your life who was like such a person?
- What are your memories of them?
- Has your knowledge of your grandparents helped you understand your parents?
- How have your grandparents shaped your life, directly or indirectly?
- Write it all down.

Silver threads

6

A feminist
is born

I think I stopped being a child when I was ten.

In Grade 4 at one of the best primary schools in my home town, I was doing well. I had incredible friends, I could read fluently and I was thriving in sports, from athletics to netball to hockey. I did exceptionally well in every sport besides swimming. I never learnt how to swim. On swimming days, the kids who couldn't swim were shoved in the shallow end of the pool to splash around, while attention was paid to all the kids who could swim, read white kids.

We were still using kickboards when they had progressed to tough strokes like butterfly. The assumption was black children don't swim, so the most the school could hope for was teaching us not to drown. It didn't seem to occur to the teachers that we couldn't swim because most of us didn't have pools. Of course, I enrolled my children in swimming lessons when they were knee-high. My four-year-old Zani is a better swimmer than both Brenden and me.

By this time, my parents were building our new house in the suburbs of Middelburg. I was ecstatic. As much as I loved our neighbourhood, I recognised that there was more. Gogo's fancy home and garden in Aerorand, and the school I attended, had enlightened me. So had my parents. Every Sunday they would drive me and my siblings around to view beautiful houses. (These days we do something similar on Pinterest, and call it manifesting.) They made sure we saw things that were bigger and better than what we had. In this way they taught us to dream.

In the days leading up to the move I told everyone what was happening and started saying my goodbyes to my neighbours on my street. Our school was not too far from our new home, so I started making friends with some of the kids who walked home. The idea of walking home from school seemed exciting at the time until it was not.

Moving day arrived.

In the history of Fridays, I am almost certain that it was the hottest of them all. From early morning the house was buzzing, glasses tinkled and slippers shuffled as my mother and aunt packed away the last few items.

Peep, peep …

Musa's taxi was right on time. That morning I had rehearsed telling the other passengers: 'Today is my last day. We are moving.'

Four years of getting to school in Musa's lime-green combi had come to an end.

That afternoon my new neighbourhood friends and I walked home together in the scorching heat, sharing stories about our day. As one by one each friend reached their house, I realised that I still had some distance to go, alone. It wasn't exciting any more. My parents had not figured out the logistics: there was no public transport, no Musa's taxi to get me home.

My dad was supposed to pick me up from school, because he was self-employed at this point and my mom was at work. More often than not, though, he couldn't make it. Getting myself home was the first of my responsibilities. There was a shortcut that all the kids took, near the train station. It reduced the journey by about two kilometres. However, I was never allowed to walk there as my mother feared for my safety. There were so many construction men walking by there, her biggest concern was that I could get raped on my way back home.

Ironically, it wouldn't be strangers I had to fear; the danger would be much closer to home. But we'll talk about that later.

Things became painful when Nonto joined our school but came out earlier, and had the peace of mind of catching a ride with our neighbour whose daughter was in the same grade. This fuelled my resentment towards her: why did I always have to tough it out, while a red carpet was rolled out for her?

When Nonto and her friend Thando reached Grade 1, we all finished school at the same time, and my transport issues were solved.

As firstborns, I don't think we acknowledge the 'figuring it out' we've experienced, from our parents literally learning how to parent with us, then having all the attention taken away from us as we watch our younger siblings have it easier, while having to be a deputy parent and still fight for the little attention our overwhelmed parents had for us.

Uncle Jack was about four years old at this time. He had his own bedroom, while I shared a room with my sister, Nonto. I didn't understand it, and I think that's where the feminist and fighter in me came alive. As respectfully as I could, and without sounding ungrateful, I asked, 'How come Mtho gets to have his own room, when I am older than him?' (Throughout our childhood, we still called Uncle Jack by his real name.)

Failing to come up with a satisfactory response, my parents gave in. I got my own room, while my sister and brother had to share theirs. My room was later painted purple, with a lilac stripe in the middle, and my photos and collages on the walls gave it personality. My room was also spotless. On weekends I would change my bedding, clean my cupboards, gather together clothes I no longer needed, which I would then give away, and move furniture around. As the firstborn I felt a need to show my sense of responsibility and enjoyment in taking care of my own space.

Like those of many families, our new home was incomplete when we moved in. No electric wires were exposed but there were no tiles, our bedroom cupboards were from our previous house and there were no kitchen cupboards or stove, only one bathroom was fully functional and our bedrooms were not painted. But we were thrilled to have more space, to have our own garden, and not to share a backyard with strangers. The house had three bedrooms but only one garage, even though my parents each had a car. When I asked about this, my mom shared that they didn't know if they would be able to afford to finish building the house, so they built just the one garage to minimise risk.

It's interesting how dreaming big can look so different from generation to generation. For my generation, the second garage would probably be a given. For my parents, building a house in which we would all be comfortable was the success – a second garage wouldn't have been as essential to them in light of what they had already achieved.

REFLECTION

I'd be lying if I said that some of these memories aren't painful. I feel sad for little Mpumi doing that long walk on her own, especially when I look at my children now and understand just how small and vulnerable they are. But I also understand that my parents were doing the best that they could with what they had.

As my therapist pointed out: 'You can love your parents with all your heart, and still be angry with them.' I really could relate to that. Despite all the not so great moments, I believe that my parents are amazing and for that reason I struggle at times to hold them accountable. And now I'm a mother myself, I know that there will be things I've done that my children will take issue with when they are older. I understand that; I accept it.

We cannot turn back the clock. All we can do is give ourselves permission to heal and do better.

- Were there moments in your childhood where you had to grow up too quickly and be the adult, even though you were still a child?
- Write those moments down.
- Think about those moments and allow yourself the chance to grieve for that young person growing up too fast. Put your arms around that younger version of yourself, and tell them everything is going to turn out better than they ever imagined.

A feminist is born

7

My first heartbreak

The first person to truly break my heart was my best friend.

I met my teenage best friend by chance. She and I knew Nonkululeko, and were invited by Noni to a gala dinner of some sort at her school. We were 14, and neither of us had fancy outfits. Her hair was a complete mess, and her mom was not having it. While Noni was getting ready for the big night, I decided to help my friend out. Shooder (a nickname) was a tomboy, and I had magic hands when it came to hair. I knew I could give her a little makeover, if she let me. That's when I got her first side-eye. I had the time of my life doing her hair; she hated the whole process.

Noni was the star of the night, while we sat awkwardly in the corner, people-watching. When I heard Shooder roar with laughter, I knew I had found my person.

For the first time in my life, I felt safe being myself around someone else. Our friendship would come to hold space for many accomplishments, adolescent firsts, tears, heartbreaks and silence.

I had found a soulmate whom I would choose over any boyfriend, and even over time spent with family.

Although we met because of a party, in truth we were home-bodies. For years, each weekend consisted of sleepovers, which then became the norm. On the weekends when she didn't come, my dad would be worried.

We cherished the moments spent in my cosy room, where we would sit on the bed and laugh all day. Friday afternoons were special – we would indulge in McDonald's foldovers, savouring each bite as we caught up on the events of the week, or cook some mince and rice before we rushed to church. Although Shooder hated cooking, her assistance was essential for us to make it to the 7 pm youth service. We appreciated the praise and worship, but seeing our crush made us even more eager to attend.

One Friday we were invited to a house party after youth service. Our outfits were pretty off. I wore pointy pumps, which one of the guys made fun of the entire night. He kept saying that he couldn't dance because he was scared I'd stab him. But I didn't care. Shooder and I had fun because we were together.

We would spend some Saturdays at her house, go to the movies or hang out at the mall hoping to meet someone we liked. For a time we dated best friends, going on double dates that consisted of just hanging out together. The guys were actually losers. No, really. The guys were actually rubbish – the one would call at like 3 am on a Friday because he said he was too busy to call during the week which would completely infuriate me. But his Zulu charm during that one phone call would keep me hanging on. These were not great romances, we just liked the attention they gave us.

We would visit Shooder's dad in Pretoria, and her mom would take us on shopping trips in Johannesburg. We learnt how to drive in her mother's pink Fiat. She attended my sports games when she could. We got our first BlackBerry phones together (remember BBM?) and attended every single family event together, whether it was a funeral, a wedding or a party; I think we even spent some Christmases together. We were inseparable.

Then everything changed.

Shooder and Romeo had been best friends as children. They had lost touch and rekindled the relationship just before our matric year. He was cute, and he found me cute. She and I had helped each other write messages to boys we liked, and with Romeo nothing was different – she gave me input on my messages to him too, I assumed. Then, with her permission, he and I started dating.

She was at a Muslim school, which didn't hold a matric dance. I had asked Romeo to be my date at mine. I suggested that they go together to his dance, so that she would have that experience. They were childhood friends, after all; I trusted her with my life. What I didn't know was that they had started developing feelings for each other.

On the day of the dance, I helped Shooder with her makeup and hair. I was even there for the photoshoot, cheering my best friend and boyfriend on. But I sensed a shift, a coolness or reserve on her part. I figured it was just nerves. With very little emotion, my best friend was slowly slipping away.

But still: 'Is everything okay?' Were they tired? Had I done something?

'We are dating now.'

Seemingly unflinchingly, she chose someone over me. Romeo pretended to be speaking to a friend, avoiding the unfolding of my heartbreak. The years of Shooder's and my friendship were reduced to a relationship that did not last.

I sometimes wonder what would have happened had she never gone to the dance.

That night I was invisible. They just wanted to be with each other, and my feelings didn't matter.

I was dropped off at home, and I cried myself to sleep.

A few months of mutual silence passed. I began to wonder whether I was making too much of it. It might have been just the heat of the moment – she didn't mean to hurt me. I was desperate to repair our friendship. I waited for her to reach out and apologise, but the call never came.

In the lead-up to prelims, I drowned my heartbreak in my studies; nothing else mattered, I was focused.

Then: 'I am so sorry.'

And: 'I didn't mean to hurt you.'

And finally: 'It was not worth it.'

I was relieved, happy to know that my best friend still cared about me. After that, we attempted to rebuild our friendship, and tried to live together at university. She was a bridesmaid at my wedding. But things had changed. She was different, I was different; we wanted different things from life. I still love her dearly, but things were never the same after that matric dance.

The last time I saw her was at her mother's funeral. I loved Shooder's mother and made sure to pay my respects. But our friendship journey had ended. I had to learn to accept that. I am starting to understand that some relationships are seasonal. That season was one of the best of my life. Shooder taught me friendship and I will always be grateful to her for that.

Letting go was hard but necessary. I experienced the greatest love and the greatest pain through our friendship.

REFLECTION

Did you have a best friend growing up? Do you remember the deliciousness of laughing with your friend until your stomach hurt? Of having someone who had your back when you were feeling awkward or ugly, or just out of place? Then maybe something happened between you, or maybe nothing happened – you just chose different subjects, or you moved to another school or town. But the friendship was never the same. Maybe you blamed yourself for the ending. Maybe it was your fault.

The only constant in life is change. We have to live in the moment, enjoying and appreciating people and experiences while we can. It's painful when things end, and the way they end can leave a bitter taste in the mouth, but remember the saying 'Don't cry because it's over, smile because it happened!'

- Write down a few memories you have of your teenage friends.
- Smile and/or cry as you remember them.
- Say thank you to the friends in your heart, or say a prayer of thanksgiving for their friendship.
- Release any bitterness or shame you may feel for how the relationship ended.

My first heartbreak

8

Angry black woman

'I am so sorry that I shouted at you so much when you were growing up.'

Exha-a-ale.

A day doesn't go by without my talking with my mother. She is one of my best friends. But it hasn't always been that way.

My childhood memories include a lot of shouting, hidings and punishment from my mother. She was an angry black woman. She was angry but she was loving, she was stressed but she showed up for everyone every single time. As her firstborn child, I got most of her rage. That's difficult for me to say, because I know the depths of her story now, parts of which only she could tell.

Like most teenage girls I have uttered the words 'I hate my mom'. With her evening bath water running, my door closed, under my bed covers and obviously under my breath.

My mother often received compliments about the smart, well-behaved and pretty girl I was.

I was always clean, my room was spotless, I would change

my bedding every Saturday morning; I cooked every Friday and soaked the dishcloths in Jik – all before the age of 15. In fact, when my older cousin Pinks moved in with us, the pressure to keep my room looking untouched turned us into enemies, after years of being close friends.

In hindsight, I realise what a tough time Pinks was going through. She had lost her dad, her mom was sick and she was sharing a room with Cleanzilla. I expected her to just get on with things, while all she probably wanted to do was lie on her bed and cry. But in the ignorance of my youth, I was blind to her pain and was being a little perfectionist to avoid being shouted at by my mom.

My first crush was Phakza. I was eight.

He was skinny and long-legged, and his head was too big for his body; he was always shining with Vaseline and as smart as they come. He sat quite close to me in class and, although he hadn't admitted it yet, I am pretty sure he had a crush on me too.

We have a beautiful love story. It could've been a dream, but I am almost certain that it happened. It was a sunny schoolday. I was dressed in my blue and white scotch tunic, with a neat hem just above the knee, bright white socks and polished shoes, minding my own business and listening to my Grade 2 teacher. I stood up to go and sharpen my pencil. You know, to keep my writing neat, crisp and on the lines. The pencil slipping out of my hand as I sat down, I dived under the table to retrieve it. And there he was, looking super nervous.

'I love you.'

Within three seconds he had whispered those potent words and hopped back into his wooden chair. *Gasp.*

That's it, that's the big love story. My heart skipped a beat, and

I waited and waited for him to ask me to be his girlfriend or show some other sign, but it never happened, and so I went home and, in the middle of my diary where nobody could ever see, I wrote 'I love PHAKZA'.

I considered whether I should now share his name or not, because we became such good friends in high school, and no doubt our group of friends will have a field day clowning on this information.

My mother found my diary. (I probably didn't hide it as well as I thought.)

She found it and she was *not happy*.

No conversation was had, no questions were asked. With a brown leather belt my mother gave me a hiding that I will never forget. She had just discovered her daughter liked someone, and her mind probably went straight to uMpumi uyajola and the how, where, when didn't matter.

Having my own daughter, I understand her shock. I remember the first time Nuri came home with the news that a boy had told her she was pretty. My maternal instinct made me want to attack, but this therapised black girl inhaled and exhaled and took it for the innocence and growth it was.

I don't know if that hiding physically hurt that much, but I know why it stands out. In that moment I remember realising that I'd have to be better at hiding my feelings and I was a bad girl for having a crush on a boy. I couldn't switch off my feelings for boys, but I did get better at lying and concealment – preserving the well-behaved girl image, at least when it came to other people. My mom, of course, always knew my business, no matter how well I tried to hide it. She didn't always acknowledge it, but I could see it in her eyes. A part of me feels like my behaviour was normal and the punishment didn't fit the crime. Whether it did or not,

I know not to get angry at my growing Nuri, but to deal with my fears first and create a safe space for her rather than turn her into a skilled pretender.

It's been difficult. My baby girl is five; I want to keep her safe and help her choose her friends. When I lose my cool, I apologise and explain why.

My mother didn't know better, and it was her way of protecting her little girl; unfortunately, it made me sneakier.

Shooder and I, as I explained, spent every weekend together. Everyone was sick of being our transport, so we started walking. We loved each other's company so much that no matter the weather, we walked to each other's houses. My mother preferred having us sleep at my house, to keep an eye on us. But there was no PVR decoder and no snacks, and I always had chores. At Shooder's there was a full-time helper, a well-stocked fridge and, of course, the PVR.

One sweltering Saturday, my best friend was visiting. We planned to spend the day at her house. But first I had to finish cleaning.

I knew my mother was not too keen on my leaving, but she had no reason to refuse us. I did the best cleaning job I could, dusting every corner and under the couches, mopping as though I was in the Shine Your Floors event at the Olympics, and finally I was done.

'Seng'hambile.'

The 40-minute walk had us sweating, and Shooder was pink in the face from sunburn but we finally made it. Her phone started ringing as we approached her gate, 'Mpumi's mom' flashing on the screen. (I didn't have a phone.) My heart sank.

'You left the mop and cleaning water in the bucket. Come back.'

'But, Mom, we just arrived and it's so hot. I'm sorry, it was a mistake …'

'I said come back.' And she hung up.

Moaning, we walked back another 40 minutes just to empty the water from the bucket and wring out the mop, my mother was that intent on teaching me a lesson.

If you've ever wondered why I finish everything I start with the same energy, it's probably because of that day.

Our relationship got better when I left home for varsity. Our conversations became honest. My mom started sharing what had been happening at that time in her life. Our hormones began to calm down. But most importantly my mother said sorry.

My mother is a safe space, a friend and a woman who apologises.

My mother is my friend and I love her.

My mother was an angry black woman.

And now, she is a healthy and loving black woman.

But it took work and an apology.

REFLECTION

We would love to blame our mothers for being too hard on us. When we look back, we realise the difficulties they were facing, and their fears about raising girl children in a world that's not particularly kind or forgiving towards girls and women.

My mother was in boarding school from the age of six. This impacted her relationship with her mother too. So I can understand why she was overprotective of me. I'm so thankful that even though my mom and I didn't always have the best relationship while I was growing up, we've worked through many of our issues and we continue to heal from things that happened at that time.

It's never too late to heal from the past but, like everything, it takes work and honesty.

What do you wish your mother or mother figure could've done better?

- If you can, have a conversation with her now using the words 'I feel' to tell her how it affected you.
- If you don't feel you can have a conversation with her, or are unable to, write her a letter telling her how she hurt you. You don't need to send the letter – you can burn it if you want to – but just writing it down helps.

9

My first flight

Birds of a feather flock together, but some may have to change their feathers. And that's the story of my life. Changing my feathers to enter rooms I have no business being in but that will lead to where I need to be. It's not a bad thing; it's the nature of life. Think about the concept of your 10 000 hours: you need to be in the right place by the time you clock those hours, or good luck putting in more time with nothing to show for it.

I became friends with the white girls in primary school, and I mean the solid white girls. Affluent families, top 10 – in fact top 5 – kind of smart, A team for hockey, netball and athletics, and easy on the eye too. This was not me. I was not white (so take away that privilege); I was happily cruising with a 60 per cent academic average, which is decent but nothing to get excited about. I made the A team for netball and did well in athletics, but oh that 90-minute squat required by the game of hockey was not my friend. Still, I eventually got on the team, and thrived. I have a good mix of hockey and netball legs to this day. But that is probably thanks more to my mom and my trainer.

I think I was in Grade 4 …

Why does it sound like everything happened to me in Grade 4? Maybe because I had hit the magical double figures in years? I don't know, but these things matter when you are young …

A part of me felt ambitious and excellent when I hung around them; even at that tender age, I knew that hanging around these girls made me want to be better.

Throughout primary school, trips were organised for each grade. My parents always made sure that I went. I realise now how much it took for them to do that.

The Grade 6 and 7 trips were announced: Durban and Cape Town.

Of course, all my friends were going to Cape Town. It was a no-brainer. With excitement, I rushed home to tell my parents that I wanted to go to Cape Town.

My dad was home earlier than usual. I could sense the tension in the air. The trip to Durban would already stretch my parents' budget but they were open to making it work. Cape Town was off the table.

I begged and begged; I promised to get higher marks, wash the dishes, do everything else I could think of. My parents didn't even stop to think about it, the answer was clear. 'We can't afford it, but Durban will be great.'

But all my friends were going to Cape Town, and I had been to Durban, so I wasn't having it. I begged even more.

Eventually: 'We will think about it.'

And they made it happen. From selling Avon products and herbal tea to doing extra marking during the holidays, my parents sacrificed to ensure not only that I got on that plane but also that I had new clothes and shoes for the trip. (Growing up, we got clothes for Christmas and winter, but for this trip my mom maxed out her Woolworths credit card and added a few cute tops from Jet.)

At 4 am, as mist enveloped the streets, my mother, Khuyu and I headed for the airport in his trusty green Toyota Corolla, driving at a steady 60 km per hour, hushed anticipation permeating the car. My stomach was churning; my parents and I had never been to the airport before, and didn't know what to expect, so Khuyu was the designated driver.

My mother looked gorgeous, as usual. Her cleavage being out didn't bother me until a friend drew attention to it behind my back.

'Look at Amanda's mom's boobs.'

For some reason, she thought my mother's breasts were an appropriate topic for 12-year-old girls to discuss, and of course news travels, so the plane had not even lifted off before I heard all the chatter.

I know now that people tend to gossip about others to feel better about themselves. At the time I was heartbroken. My mom was and is a very attractive woman, but somehow they turned that into something ugly.

Feeling like an outsider on a school trip we could barely afford, I had to worry about what others thought about my mother as well.

As if that wasn't enough: 'I hope I get the window seat.'

'The aisle is my favourite.'

'What about you, Amanda, have you been on a flight before?'

And in that moment my little 12-year-old brain had to choose, do I flock with these birds or will I be the outsider who's never been on a plane before? You guessed it, I lied. I lied and I regretted it because the minute I opened my mouth I knew that nobody believed me.

'Yes, I went to Cape Town for my grandmother's sister's funeral. On a plane.'

Really? Was that the best I could do?

What else was I supposed to say? I didn't know a thing about window seats, and other than Durban and Cape Town, where did flights go? The topic immediately changed, which is how I knew my lie was bad.

As soon as we were seated, everybody buckled their seatbelts, not waiting for the flight attendant to give instructions. I tried to do the same, but if you know that seatbelt, you know: you kind of have to know what you are doing.

I lied about my first flight because I didn't want pity. I lied about Cape Town because I wanted to fit in. In hindsight I robbed myself of a beautiful first-time experience because I wanted to feel part of the gang. And that's what I love about growing up: although I still sometimes put on different wings to flock with birds who are doing incredible things, I no longer lie. I own my firsts and gladly ask for help on how to buckle my seatbelt.

Dear reader, if anything, I hope you know that becoming the best version of yourself will come with discomfort, and acquainting yourself with people who are already where you want to be.

In the end, the Cape Town trip was a blast. It didn't matter that I had never been on a flight. I discovered what sitting in a window seat felt like, and I've been choosing it ever since.

By the time we parted ways to go to high school, I had caught up. My marks were higher, I was one of two black prefects, I finally convinced my parents to get DStv so I could watch *Hannah Montana*, but more importantly I had experienced a connection with incredible girls from different backgrounds.

All of them are doing amazingly well. One lives in my neighbourhood, another completed her MBA at 26. Funnily enough, we recently bumped into each other at the airport – I on my way to Dubai, she off to Singapore. As we caught up, I realised that Ashley may never know how much her friendship opened up my world. Her mother was my teacher and netball coach. That woman affirmed everything in me. I can still see her bright eyes, her curly brown hair … She always called me by my name, looked me in the eye and told me how special I was.

Thank you, Mrs Baldwin, for giving me permission to shine in rooms and spaces that were not intended for a little black girl.

REFLECTION

I can guarantee you that even the most privileged, richest, best-looking person in the world has had a moment in their lives where they felt like they didn't fit in. Some people are just better at hiding it than others – and you would never know that they were feeling awkward or uncomfortable.

I'm not sure if this experience had something to do with it but, to this day, the one thing I don't do is lie. I don't even tell white lies. I would rather say nothing than let a lie pass my lips.

- What is something you lied about in an attempt to fit in?
- Or maybe you made fun of someone else who didn't come from the same background as you. Perhaps you passed on gossip that in retrospect you should've kept quiet about.
- When you look back now, how do you wish you had handled it?
- Write it down.

PART TWO
I am
the magic

10

Chosen

'I am not feeling well.'

And with that, my journey with accounting and university ended.

If you believe you are worthy, half the job is done.

Most people don't believe they are worthy of good things. I get it. Well, sort of. Half of me doesn't get it because I think I deserve all good things, but the other half understands because I know that not everyone grew up in an environment that was as affirming and supportive as mine.

I was in Grade 8, excited about life, filled with emotion and took everything to heart. The night before one of our accounting tests, I studied really hard. I didn't want to feel left out. My circle of friends was smart and hardworking; naughty too, but our marks made up for it. I felt confident; I had prepared and written with ease. I was pretty sure I had a good 75 per cent waiting for me.

With a stern, unfriendly, Afrikaans accent, the teacher called out our names with our marks while handing out our papers. I confidently waited for mine as my friends got 80s and 90s …

'Amanda, 43.'

And so my revenge journey of almost seven years started.

It's why I got a distinction in matric; well, almost – 79 per cent in accounting. (Khuyu suggested I get a re-mark for that single per cent.) It's why I chose to take accounting at varsity, gaining a bursary, distinctions and even a job leading there. But my career choice was not well thought-out. That day in that classroom, I burst into tears of shame and humiliation. Worse was the overachieving monster it awakened in me. I set out to prove to everyone that I wasn't just some dumb, pretty girl.

Finding my feet in Joburg was a challenge, in hindsight. At the time I did not see myself as a girl from a small town trying to make it in the big city. When choosing a university I knew that Johannesburg was the place where I would make my dreams come true.

During this time, I made relationships that would help me once I was out of varsity. I diligently served at church and built a community there. One member of our church, who used to help me when my car got stuck, remains a close family friend to this day. I worked for multiple promotion companies and became a number-one candidate whenever there was a big job.

When my parents dropped me off at res, while squashed in his little four-ton truck together with my mother, my dad pointed towards Campus Square shopping centre and said, 'If you fool around, you will work here.' As if working at Campus Square would be the worst thing that could happen to a person. I didn't exactly fool around or finish, and I never worked at one of the shops there, but I did have a billboard at Campus Square.

After I dropped out of varsity, my neighbour recommended me to his modelling agency. I met with the owner and was signed on the spot. Having landed my first audition, I secured the campaign and worked with the Mukheli brothers while they were building their brand. Some time later, I had Justice on my podcast, and Fhatuwani graciously allowed Nuri, a budding artist, into his studio. It felt like a full-circle moment. I also have some of Fhatuwani's incredible art in my house.

Three more auditions and I realised modelling was not for me. I was surrounded by better-looking and more stylish people, which made me feel insecure. I do not believe in staying in places that make me question who I am, so that was the end of that.

The best things the University of Johannesburg gifted me were friendship, a husband and a work ethic. I met Dee outside class. I ran to the bathroom to cry about something. (I know I am in an emotionally healthy space when I cry a lot – when I allow myself to express my feelings in this way without pretending to be strong.) Dee was with a few people, and we immediately hit it off. We were a group of five very different people but we would stick together, and Dee, Sizwe and I became inseparable. We needed each other and would go through varsity anchoring each other. Sizwe's life was way more exciting than ours: he had a taste for fun and he was a genius. He would study on the morning of a test using our notes and sometimes do better than us!

Every year, I would tell Dee how much I didn't want to pursue accounting. The conversation was usually sparked by her enthusiasm for her well-thought-out career path, while I was preoccupied by the money I was going to earn and the music career I envisioned. Each time, she would encourage me to keep going, yet leave room for me to imagine a life outside what felt like a prison to me.

At the end of the first semester of third year, I listened to my innate desire to follow my gut no matter what. It was Monday afternoon; after a weekend of studying, I was fully prepared and looking forward to my finance exam. Usually Dee and I would drive to varsity together, in my red Yaris. This time, Dee being ill, I was alone. Everything else was normal until the moment the invigilator said, 'You may start.'

The pages in front of me went blank; my mind transported me to a world where I was free, a world where I was 'ministering' (without clearly showing me what that looked like). I kept trying to bring my thoughts back, to focus on the exam, but it was useless. I knew I was done.

But all I said was: 'I am not feeling well; I'll write another day.'

I grabbed my things, jumped into my car and called my mother, wailing as I struggled to explain what had just happened.

Gogo was listening in and insisted that I was merely tired and needed to eat some fish. In other words, I just needed some brain food in the form of Omega-3. I hated disappointing my gran, but oily fish was not going fix this. So, I packed a small bag, got on the highway and played Tasha Cobbs Leonard's 'Immediately' the whole way home with tears running down my face. Those were tears of relief, trust and knowing what I did was right, but also tears of fear: what next?

I had no real plan. I left to avoid seeing how upset my parents would be, which would have made me doubt my decision. I knew in my heart God was the reason I left that exam room. I had to prove I wasn't mistaken. I desperately wanted to succeed, to achieve something, anything … because I knew that everyone was waiting to see this God thing happen.

It didn't happen as I thought.

But I have no doubt that I am living in God's dream for me. I have always felt that I was chosen, that I am unique. My husband often tells me how special I am, confirming a belief I have carried with me since I was young. Sometimes I wonder if every child starts off like this, only for life's challenges to chip away at that belief, which just a few manage to hold on to.

There are so many people who would be better, I feel, at doing what I do. People who are less stubborn, pray more, memorise verses better, have more empathy and are simply more talented than I am. Yet God somehow decided I am the one for this.

I am not extremely insecure or fearful, or ungrateful. My sense of inadequacy lies at the heart of my entreaty to God: *if you don't come through, I will humiliate both of us.* Before any speaking engagement, or podcast, or suchlike, I silently speak Luke 12:12: 'For the Holy Spirit will teach you in that very hour what you ought to say.'

And that gives me peace. Because God has sent me, He will give me the words to speak, and so far He has been faithful. I have never doubted that I am destined for amazing things, whether it was being a dermatologist, as I expressed in my Grade 4 speech, or an actress or designer, and for the longest time, a gospel singer.

At 13 I wanted to be Joyce Meyer. I would watch her sermons every night and preach at cell meetings on Wednesday evenings. I don't think I wanted to be a preacher, but I saw a woman with a voice and the courage to be herself, and that resonated with me. I knew that I was that girl.

My parents played a major role in my self-awareness. Whatever passion I chose, they invested in it. When I wanted to play sports, my mother sacrificed her last few rands to get me the best New Balance tackies for the netball court and attended almost every game, which I played up to provincial level.

When she noticed I had a gift for public speaking, she got me extra lessons with my speech and drama teacher. In my young eyes Mrs Fraserbel appeared to be very old, but she was probably around 70. She was always smartly dressed in a blazer, and maintained excellent posture. Every Wednesday afternoon I would have a session with her that seemed endless but was in fact only an hour long. She was very focused on teaching me the intricacies of body language, storytelling and commanding a room. She would meticulously guide me on how to lift my shoulders, open my mouth effectively and share engaging stories. It was a challenging but valuable experience. Because I knew what she liked, I would kill the Monday drama classes at school, unlike others whose poor grammar would earn them a tongue-lashing.

Sadly, Mrs Fraserbel never got to see me flourish from those seeds she planted in me, but I will always remember what she taught me. Sometimes when I'm about to give a speech I hear her voice in my head telling me to stand up straight and sound my vowels.

Besides drama and netball, there were also my short-lived stints as a magazine editor and fashion designer. I once spent an entire afternoon on my dad's computer, laying out my magazine with Oprah on the cover. I used magazines and my famous Oxford dictionary to do my research.

When a sudden interest in design came about, in true Mpoomy style – I should now say in Nuri and Zani style – I was consumed. Every moment I had, I would whip out my sketch pad and draw.

One dress stood out to my dad. The top part was rectangular with a pocket in front. The sleeves, or lack thereof, gave it a delela (dungarees) vibe. From the waist, it went down to cover my feet. I think I was in my Rastafarian era! I guess the sketch was so good that my dad decided this was it. We visualised the look: it would be denim, with a bright mustard-coloured long-sleeved top underneath and my white Converse All Stars that Boocy had gifted me.

My dad took me to the fabric shop to pick out the denim. For some reason we picked the stiffest denim there was, and off we went to a small, shady-looking Indian workshop to find a tailor. We chose a beautiful mustard thread that matched my Legit top and we were set.

The tailor did an amazing job. I could not walk in my dress, but I didn't let that hold me back: I wore it to church and felt like The Girl even as I shuffled to my seat.

That moment was bigger than the dress; it was about the belief my dad had in me. That moment taught me these things: if we can dream it, think it or imagine it, we can have it; dreams are nothing without hard work; and whatever I try, something good will come of it.

From the age of four, I would join my dad on stage and lead our Sunday school in song. So, yes, I have always been self-confident, but my parents made it their mission to ensure that I lived up to that success-related name of mine, Nompumelelo.

I tell this story every chance I get, mostly to parents and for adults who never received that affirmation to understand where their thinking and belief patterns come from. It matters that we express interest when our children show us something. We need to make sure that they know that anything is possible.

First, we dream, then we put in the work and keep trying until we find that which speaks to our souls.

Over time, I have changed my mind a lot. I have worked in the corporate arena, own a beauty salon, have been a backup vocalist for gospel singer Dr Tumi, am an influencer, have a YouTube channel, have a podcast and a wellness hub. And I've written this book. Who knows what's next?

Whatever it is, it will work out, because I – not it – am the magic.

REFLECTION

Words are powerful and have a significant impact on our lives. They can be compared to seeds that are planted during our journey. The seeds that are nurtured and watered have the potential to grow and flourish. Therefore, let us make a conscious effort to sow seeds of affirmation, encouragement, joy and support in the lives of our children.

We should also be vigilant in identifying and uprooting any negative seeds that may have been inadvertently sown, and instead cultivate a fresh garden of positivity and magic in our lives.

- What did you dream of being when you were a child?
- When you told people what you wanted to be, how did they respond?
- How did their response affect you?
- What does your inner voice sound like? Is it a kind, encouraging voice, or is it a mean voice, like that of a teacher who may have told you you would never amount to anything?
- If you have a mean inner voice, you will have to work to change the way you speak to yourself. The first step is listening to what the voice says. Then identify where that voice comes from. Is it your father, a horrible teacher or a sadistic sports coach? Finally, respond to the mean voice. When it tells you you're stupid, list all the reasons why you are not stupid.
- From now on, speak to yourself as you would speak to the person you love most in the world. Yes, fam, that's you! You need to love yourself before you can love anyone else.
- Write it all down.

11

I quit!

Ten minutes with my kids is enough to show the kind of child I was.

Some time ago, Brenden and I excitedly told our children that we were going to Durban. It would be our son's first flight.

But: 'Why not Paris?'

In that moment, I understood what my parents had had to deal with. I don't know if it's inherited or learnt. While through their actions my parents indicated that there is more to life, they did not tell me outright that I should be successful. I certainly didn't tell my children about Paris; what I do teach them is that they should never settle, especially my daughter because, as she grows, I know people will expect her value to be attached to serving others.

That's why I am a feminist. Not because I want to start 'burning my bra' (one of the biggest misconceptions about feminism), but because I strongly believe that men and women should be treated equally. While Brenden is expected to go after his dreams and gets applauded for doing whatever it takes to get ahead, including compromising time with family, I am expected to sacrifice my dreams to make sure that there's always milk and bread, toilet paper, a home-cooked meal and a freshly ironed shirt for him. I find great value in serving others, but it shouldn't be my – or any woman's – identity.

My dad is a feminist too, I think. He was raised by a woman who was, to all intents and purposes, single. While my grandfather was away working for months at a time, my grandmother had to be the head of the household. Knowing the feeler that my dad is, I am almost certain that seeing his mother struggle to make ends meet encouraged him to empower his children, boys and girls alike. I have always had a job. I like money, and I don't like asking for it.

'But dad, it's school holidays!' June school holidays to be exact. And this was before climate change kicked in, so winter was freezing.

'You have five minutes.'

No time for a bath, I brushed my teeth, slathered myself with lotion on the parts that were not covered by my thick clothes, layered on socks, vest, scarf and a beanie, and off I went.

I still carry that with me. It's 5 am as I write this, my family is sleeping; this is the only time I have for writing.

I made tea … not this morning … at my dad's office. That was my job, I made tea for him, and it bored me senseless. Usually the first to arrive, we would open the office and I would make his first cup of tea. As soon as the rest of the staff arrived, he was off and I would be at the office until he came back to pick me up at 5 pm.

You read that right: I would leave home early to go to make one cup of tea … and spend the next several hours at an office doing, effectively, nothing. Did I want to go home earlier? Of course. Is that how jobs work? Absolutely not. All that time spent there played a part in forming my career. I knew I wanted to be the boss because the thought of staying in one place and doing the same thing every day drove me crazy.

The mistake I made was failing to negotiate my pay before starting. When pay day arrived, I was elated. My sacrifice of my holidays, and my perception of myself as a hard worker, in contrast to my siblings who stayed at home, was going to be rewarded.

My dad gave me R100.

Thinking back, it was a decent amount, considering my age and the time. But I was fuming. I didn't do much, but I had given up my time, which seemed worth more to me than R100. In frustration, I wrote my dad a letter on a piece of white paper in big bold letters:

I QUIT.

It's now a joke in the family that my dad paid me so little I resigned on the spot. This wouldn't be the last time I worked for him, but it was certainly the last time I did so without first negotiating my fee and hours.

I got my next job at 16. My best friend and I walked to the new shopping centre in our area, and I applied for a job at Spur. I was so nervous, because I knew I would be the youngest person there. In the days leading up to the final test, I spent a lot of time studying the menu and learnt the word 'schnitzel'. I aced the test and got the job.

Now I realise that there were people who needed the job more than I did, but who didn't get it. But I don't think we talk enough about the importance of having confidence – in what we say and how we speak. We don't want to admit it but articulation and good command of English matter, because we need to be proud of our language and not put English on a pedestal, but English put herself on the pedestal and she is not giving it up easily.

As waitrons we wore dark blue jeans and a Spur shirt, a uniform I had to complete with a second-hand orange hoodie; it was giving

Prison Break vibes. I hated working there but my tips were good, so I stuck it out.

On what would turn out to be my worst day, an old white couple came to have their lunch. What I didn't know is that they were regulars, and nobody wanted to serve them. Nobody except Grace and Peter, a wonderful couple from Zimbabwe. But they were both swamped, so I had to step up. My confident self thought it would be easy, I would just have to be extra polite.

They ate their entire meal, leaving their plates clean, and proceeded to ask for the manager. I can still smell the racism on them; my heart beats a little faster when I think of those 40 minutes I spent serving a couple who thought that I – a bright 16-year-old girl, with a better twang than they had – belonged in the kitchen and at their mercy.

Grace eventually took over the table, as I had to go to the back room to cry. I thought I was upset because I messed up an order and ended up having to pay for it. But I was crying because the couple made me feel smaller than the woman's off-white pearl earrings.

After that incident, I promised myself that no white person would ever walk over me again. My mom and dad had made sure I always knew my value and worth. And I no longer allow people to question it. I have a bit of a bull terrier living in me – she comes out when my worth is questioned.

My willingness to do any job has helped me accumulate experience. I have worked for my dad multiple times. Even in my first year of marriage, for extra money, I would work in my dad's office about three days of the week, while studying towards a beauty diploma, practising my nail art skills on him and the other office staff. I have sung for money, but after my gig with Dr Tumi – although a dream come true and an incredible learning experience that paid well – I knew that being a musician was not sustainable for the type of life I desired. At the top of my list for my life's goals were freedom and comfort. But these don't happen without putting in time and effort. I was lucky to learn that it wasn't just going to fall into my lap – not only from listening to what my parents said, but from watching how they worked so hard for everything.

As someone who has been vilified for quitting, be it friendships, jobs or the Pilates class that didn't bring me joy, I think it's okay to do so when your self-worth is being questioned. It will require something a little more complicated than scribbling your message on a piece of white paper, but there's always a way out to save yourself.

REFLECTION

It's very rare these days that a person works in one job for 30 years, gets their gold watch and retires. We're all hustlers now. Think about your own work situation and write down all the jobs you've had, from that first job cleaning for cash or making vetkoek to whatever you're doing now.

- What was it about each job that made you realise it wasn't for you?
- What skills did you learn from each job?
- When you look back, can you see how each job was a step on the path to where you are now?
- Where would you like to be?
- What would you still like to achieve?
- Write it down.

I quit!

12

Stepping stones

Let me tell you about Pastor Steven Furtick …

My best friend Dee and I were focused girls. While at varsity, we tried the going-out-and-living-our-best-lives thing. It just wasn't us. To this day, I've been to a club only once, and it wasn't with Dee. I was overdressed in jeans and a leather jacket, and I stayed in the bathroom all night watching pretty drunk girls in skimpy dresses throw up or fix their makeup.

Instead, our downtime was a day spent indoors with Chicken Licken Party 16 and *Being Mary Jane* or some other show Dee was into, while I napped on her bed. When we both started working and had less time to spend together, I would drop my laptop off at her place, and she would add a new downloaded series or movie (this was before Netflix and streaming services), and one day, she added a sermon by Pastor Steven Furtick preaching at his church, Elevation.

I didn't watch this sermon until about a year later, when I had dropped out. Brenden and I were chilling in my little cottage in the south of Joburg. During that time I didn't know whether I was going or coming. Each day was a surprise; each day I hoped to get a life-changing phone call, from whom I don't know. I was building an ark not knowing when the rain was coming.

One morning, Brenden came across the sermon on my laptop. It was the first kernel of change in our lives. For Brenden the significance lay in seeing a pastor who dressed like him: black T-shirt, sneakers and jeans. After years of attending church, religion was something he needed a break from. But when Pastor Furtick offered us a relationship with Christ instead of the dos and don'ts of Christianity, a seed was sown. In fact, he is one of the reasons we do what we do.

The foundation of our work is that we want people to get to know Jesus, the lover, Father and kind shepherd he is, and in his love they may walk in their purposes. We don't preach from a pulpit, but through our platforms and everyday interactions we hope that God's love radiates in the simplest way, as it did for us through Pastor Furtick. We realised that God's love is not dressed up in a costume; He made us and loves us as we are, with all our differences, and there is room for all of us to be ourselves.

Pastor Steven was the glue we needed to hold us together in that space of uncertainty.

Have you ever had nothing to wake up for except that WhatsApp group, or that friend, boyfriend or person? That was Brenden and me. Our relationship was the only thing we had. Let me tell you how it all began ...

I started university in 2013, filled with excitement at being the first in my dad's family to do so. That year Brenden also left Mpumalanga to study music, or rather to use that as his gateway to Gauteng to enter one of the biggest music competition shows, *Idols*. In case you are wondering, I didn't get to see his season, because I didn't have a TV.

I was also very intentional about serving at church and building relationships there, which is how I met Mahalia Buchanan, who became an older sister and role model during my time at varsity and as a newbie in Joburg. Among other things she introduced me to Twitter, and told me to follow this really cute guy who would turn out to be my husband.

Thinking nothing of it, I continued my life and my studies, and being a celibate queen. Okay, maybe not completely celibate; let's just say, I was in my celibacy era, but I wasn't always consistent.

Just before the June holidays, Dee and I were pulling an all-nighter preparing for our semester exams. We studied to the sounds of The DJ Man on Metro FM. That night he introduced 'All of Me' by John Legend. As a huge John Legend fan I was in heaven, and blown away by the beauty of the words and the melody, and how the song made me feel.

I told Dee, 'The guy I'm going to marry is going to sing that song to me!'

As life would have it, the first time I finally watched *Idols*, during the holidays, Brenden performed … you guessed it … 'All of Me'. And, very casually, I told my mom I was going to marry this guy.

Our relationship began as a friendship between two 19-year-olds who grew up in small towns with dreams that far exceeded our surroundings. He was the first man I knew who didn't limit my dreams and beliefs. In our first two-hour phone call (courtesy of Dee and Brenden's Cell C contracts, which allowed us to talk for free), we connected over the most random things, and I willingly gave up studying time to get to know this superstar.

Dee, though, wasn't too thrilled by him. 'Uzenza uChris Brown.' And: 'Uzenza icheeses.' (Implying that he was arrogant.)

We didn't date until a year after that initial conversation. We had spoken on the phone now and then, until I had withdrawn from him, having concluded that Dee was right – he was on the arrogant side.

Around June of 2014, I was invited to a youth concert, and he happened to be performing there. If you are a Steve Harvey fan, you know what he used to say about a woman in white jeans. I stepped out of my old Toyota Yaris, in my tight white jeans, checked shirt and soft dreads, to find that Brenden, having parked right next to me, had just got out of his car. He froze in awe, and later shared that he couldn't believe I was real.

And that is how we met. Nothing fancy, no planned date, simply a chance meeting after we had lost touch. That day solidified our relationship, not just as people in love but as soulmates who would carry each other no matter what.

A few months later, we decided to be together. Brenden had not found his footing in his career and depended on gigs that would come by chance (though there never was a month when he didn't have a gig). I had just started my cleaning business and registered for a business course at Rosebank College. I needed to be in Joburg and this was the only way, I thought, I could get my parents to pay for it. But my dad knew exactly what I was up to, and refused to pay for me to stay in my cosy two-bedroom flat at The Yard in Auckland Park. So I moved into a tiny garden cottage in the south of Joburg. It was probably the size of my home office now. The couple who owned the property were cold towards each other, it seemed to me at the time, and I judged them for it. Now that I've been married for over seven years, I understand. Nothing will humble you like the seven-year itch, but more on that later.

As for my business course, I need to pay my mother back for wasting her money, because I attended just a few times. I had done the work in my accounting course at varsity, and all I would do was travel from the south to Braamfontein to mark the register, until I met a friend who would do it for me. Showing up only to write tests and exams, I still managed to be at the top of the class. I stopped attending altogether. What I had really needed was to buy myself time to figure out what I wanted to do next, and in that sense it was a success.

Brenden had moved back home to Graskop, to try to get back on his feet and create music. But we were in love, and we needed each other.

Dee and I had remained friends, but the shame of no longer being at varsity, and living so far away and having no solid life plan made me start to withdraw. This is a thing I do when I feel stuck. Hating the idea of being a burden, I retreat to figure myself out. I'm well aware that this is not the way to have genuine, meaningful friendships.

Brenden used to visit me at least once a week. After a while, he started to feel that it was becoming too expensive for him to keep making the journey. We convinced ourselves that the best opportunities were in Joburg, and he was wasting money by going home, and I was alway borrowing his car because mine kept breaking down. He needed a place to stay, and I needed to borrow his Polo, which he had bought with some of his *Idols* money. So we kind of moved in together. And every time my parents came to visit, he would grab his bag and go and wait at the nearest garage.

Girl, the guilt was real.

I was fully serving in the worship team at church, and he is a pastor's child. After being celibate for a year, we foreplayed our way into sex. We would repent every time in the hope that it would never happen again. It did. It felt wrong and we knew it.

One winter afternoon we were shopping at our local Woolies.

Hand in hand, we had one of those cloud nine debates about which vegetables to get. Amused by our conversation, a middle-aged couple approached us.

The husband said, 'Would you like to join our married couples' group? I love how you treat each other. There are many couples and activities you can learn from.'

'Thanks, but we're not married,' we giggled.

Convinced that we would be married soon, he wouldn't take no for an answer. Brenden and I had already discussed marriage, especially since we were having sex. I don't know how bad it was for Brenden, but I believed I was going straight to hell.

We joined the group, which as we'd been told was filled with couples. I sent the pamphlet for my new cleaning business to the WhatsApp group, and got a great response. With this client base and diligent work, I became very busy and had to recruit more women to assist me.

I also started making enough money from all my jobs to fix my Yaris. I told my dad, but he suggested that I just buy a new car, and he would help me with a deposit. I could finally get my dream car, a white Hyundai Grand i10.

The deposit brought the instalments to a more or less comfortable level, and I never skipped a payment. Buying that car was a big step towards the faith-filled life I was intent on living.

Brenden was offered a job at a church in Little Falls that would pay him enough money to get his own place and be comfortable. After a year of hard work, things were finally shaping up for both of us. It felt like the break we had been praying for.

Brenden moved to the west, and I moved closer to him. One of the couples in the church group was looking for an au pair with the offer of a decent, consistent salary of R3 000 a month.

I had the cleaning business, I worked as an au pair and I

continued to do the promotional jobs that I had begun to do while at varsity. For one of the promotional projects I made about R15 000, which was huge at the time.

Because the house I au paired at was closer to Brenden, I was now always at his place. He was living in a back room in a house in which some bachelors who loved his music lived. It was a bit awkward voting for someone on TV, being a fan and renting a back room with them. But we got used to it. The room was even smaller than the one I had had in the south, but I got him decent bedding, cooked good meals and made it into a home. I was sharing a gorgeous two-bedroom flat in Northriding, but his place was cosier.

Every day he would drop me off at my client's workplace. In her BMW, Lebo Sekgobela playing on the sound system, I would pick up her little daughter, sit with her while she ate a meal and take her to play at her grandmother's house in Dainfern. My client was a doctor, her husband was an accountant and her parents were a doctor and an engineer. The exposure to their wealth, ambition and belief in Christ had me fired up. I didn't like the job but I loved the couple.

REFLECTION

I don't believe in coincidences. Every phase of my life has been necessary and has presented me with a lesson. Things that you have gone through – changes, seasons, careers – that you may not have thought to be relevant actually are. Everything is leading you to where you are supposed to go and to who you are supposed to be. But you have to learn the lesson – whichever lesson life is throwing at you – otherwise you stay *stuck*.

Look at the bad patterns you may have repeated ...
- Can you identify moments where you repeated patterns that hindered your growth?
- Perhaps you kept on dating the same kind of person who did not want the same things you did?
- Or you hung around with the wrong crowd that wasn't allowing you to reach your full potential?
- Maybe you kept spending money you didn't have on things you didn't need?
- Do you see any of those patterns in your own life?
- Write them down.

Now flip the coin: look at the good patterns you've repeated ...
- Perhaps you've been consistent about exercising or self-care?
- Maybe you're great about keeping promises and keeping in touch with friends?
- Or you could be great at saving or are excellent at your job?
- Write it all down!

13

Perfect is
not perfect

Fast forward to a year later, and Brenden and I were married.
Yes, we'll talk about the wedding and all the jazz, but first, let
me tell you about my salon.

After receiving my beauty diploma, I opened a mobile nail bar
called Aneno. As I got better and my client list grew, I employed
more nail technicians and soon we had a salon. It was thriving.
We were fully booked almost every day, and we were slowly out-
growing our small property. 'Property' sounds fancy; in reality, it
was a room rented from an old woman whose husband had left
her a house in Melville that she could no longer afford. So she
turned her garage into a usable space, and the minute I saw it I
was sold. The space was far from glamorous, but it was right on
the road and next to incredible restaurants.

I saw the salon as I see people: as projects with potential. This
can be toxic, I know; I am working on it. Whether it is toxic
or is a beautiful way to see things, it has gotten me burnt. Not
everybody wants to be better, and you can turn blue in the face

showing them their potential – if they don't want to do the work, it ain't happening.

Anyway, I had saved up some money from all the house calls I was doing, but it still wasn't enough. Being the businesswoman I am, I drew up a business plan, figures and all, from a Google template, and set up a meeting with my dad. One Friday evening I sat down after supper to present this plan to him in order to ask him for a loan. My heart pounding, I talked too fast and sounded like a heavy breather on a nuisance call. But I was convincing. After a few questions on how I would make the money and pay it back, my dad agreed to loan me R80 000.

Mahalia possesses a natural creative talent and has always been passionate about design and creating visually appealing spaces. Together, we threw ourselves into the task of transforming the room into a salon, all the while meticulously planning the grand opening night. On that night, some special people in my life showed up, and my mother gave me eight sumptuously soft, high-quality towels – an example of the love and affirmation I received from her. Knowing she had my back made me feel safe and encouraged me to keep striving. In this case, the reason for the white towels was clear: she expected a spotless space. I made sure to keep it that way.

After a few months, I was ready to repay the loan. My dad, however, firmly replied, 'No. Use that money to grow your business.'

This was my big break. My salon was no longer for survival and income; it was time for me to be a serious businesswoman, with vision. Although I never paid back the loan – not for lack of trying.

It was time to move.

I had money, but not enough. I have come to know that that will always be the case: the vision will always be bigger than the funds. But if it's from God, and you are faithful with the daily steps, He will provide for the vision He gave you, as long as you don't sit on it. After a few years of trying to get funding, I finally received approval. I won't even go into what a gruesome process it was, all the documents that had to be filled in, the daily trips to the National Youth Development Agency and the waiting period. As soon as we secured our spot at 27 Boxes, a new and upcoming complex, we were ready to shopfit, and this time I was going to use a professional company.

We discussed everything – timelines, budget, the works – and I put in notice with Mandy, our landlord, and announced that we were moving to bigger and better.

The work began. Or, at least, the contractor pretended to begin. I was about 24 then, and naive – I took his word for it. He had me convinced that all the parts were being created in his workshop and they would be put together at a later stage. Every day I went to check on his progress to find that the space was filled with dust and little else. Bad news for my thriving salon. The opening event was planned and announced, this time with some of the biggest celebrities and influencers I knew. I wanted to reach more people for this bigger and better space, and I knew what sharing their experience with their followers would do.

There's faith, then there's me.

On the day of the opening night, I walked into our store. The dust had not been cleared and the construction team were simply sitting around, waiting. I burst into tears. Brenden went to have it out with the project manager, throwing a few f-bombs around. Returning to me, he said, 'Babe, I don't think we can open tonight.'

Being me, I told him he needed to be positive and we just had to believe; there was still time for something to be done. Spoiler alert: it took another two weeks to finish. But in that moment I genuinely believed that things could be pulled together.

I chuckle at the craziness now, but it's what makes me *me*. I can see beyond the rough edges; I believe I can make things work.

I didn't cancel the event, but at 6 pm I did give up thinking everything would magically be finished. My guests – including my friend Thabiso, clutching a bunch of flowers – started arriving, followed by my mom and dad, who had driven all the way from Middelburg in their finery to see … a construction site. All I could do was burst into a million more tears – of humiliation, and disappointment, and a feeling of failure. Vongai, an amazing makeup artist, took charge. She contacted everyone who was still on their way to inform them that the event was postponed. It was not her job, we were not that close, but she handled that night, the clean-up, clearing up after and the staff the following week, while I drove home to hide in my bedroom and cry. Sibu Mabena, the incredible businesswoman who had agreed to deliver a short speech that evening, called to ask if she could deliver a gift to my house. As I was too broken to face anyone, Brenden fetched it: a book called *The 5AM Club*, which contained words that would change the trajectory of my career and my lifestyle.

That next week, I started therapy and I realised something: perfectionism had almost driven me mad.

REFLECTION

There is a saying about writing that goes something like this: 'You can't edit a blank page.' Authors (hey, that's me too now!) also like to talk about the sh*tty first draft.

What this means is that you have to start somewhere, and that your first attempt at whatever you're trying to create is not going to be perfect. With that in mind, think about your own life ...

- When have you allowed your perfectionism to stop you from moving forward?
- Write it down.
- Have you noticed in your life that when you release things they turn out so much better? Think back to occasions where that happened.
- Write them all down.

14

You can't
google cows

R 10 000. That was our wedding budget.

We were living together.

Christian, unmarried and nobody knew. I had my flat and
he had his own place, but we spent most of our time with each
other – cohabiting without making it official.

Brenden and I had been discussing marriage, so I decided to
talk to my mother about it. Suspecting the truth, having married
at a young age and loving Brenden, she was not opposed to the
idea. Brenden's parents, on the other hand, loved me but thought
that at 22 we could wait a bit. Our minds were made up, however,
and they gave us their blessing.

I didn't believe in lobola at the time – I just wanted to marry
the love of my life and start our lives – but I knew it would be
a big deal for my dad.

Arriving at my parents' house, Brenden spent almost an hour
standing outside, terrified of my father. Eventually, he gathered

the courage to come in and, although I can't recall exactly what was said, I do remember how brief and awkward the conversation was.

My dad was happy for us to marry on condition that Brenden pay lobola.

Not in cash but with real cows.

Real cows, like *mooo*!

I was hoping an engagement and a small wedding would suffice, but my dad was adamant that cows would make him happy.

Two live cows and about R7 000 or so in cash.

With the festive season coming up, Brenden was confident that he would make the money. He was booked for a few gigs, the lobola process could begin and we set a date for January. As soon as we shared the date with my parents, all the gigs were cancelled. I mean *all* of them. I took it as a sign that our faith was being tested, and, really, it was.

But as we held on and trusted God, a friend of my dad's booked Brenden to perform at the Christmas parties of various departments at his workplace, of which he ended up doing about five (he was that good). The earnings from these and the family weddings he was booked for that December meant he could pay my lobola. It became a standing joke that Bab'Nani and all his departmental parties paid for my lobola in full!

In Zulu culture, the letter of intent comes first. This handwritten letter from the family requests permission to build relations and a date for negotiations to begin. Brenden's older sister and her husband brought the letter to my parents. I sat there awkwardly, as though I didn't know these people (despite their being the first relatives Brenden introduced me to). Once that was over, the lobola planning started.

I had done everything I could to convince my dad that he

didn't need walking cows – money would be a better investment. But he had just bought a farm, so it made sense to him to get some cows. Brenden felt like my dad was challenging him, and I understand why. Imagine being 22 and searching for cows? 'You can't google cows!' he said. Eventually, his sister's husband, who was the chief negotiator, found the cows and everyone was happy.

Throughout December, wedding preparations consumed much of our time and energy. My attention was divided as I spent half of the month in Johannesburg, making extra money and searching for the perfect flat for us to begin our new life together.

I sensed the proposal coming. Brenden has a tell when he's about to surprise me, asking too many questions, smiling a little too much and being unable to sit still. To avoid ruining the surprise and disappointing him, I have to pretend not to notice. Seven years in and nothing's changed.

One morning he requested that I have my nails fixed. I always have my nails done, but he insisted that I get a fresh set. And: 'We are going to dinner tonight at my sister's house – look cute.'

Easier said than done. I had absolutely nothing to wear except a short floral dress and sandals.

On the drive, my mind was filled with a million questions. We arrived to the dinner table set for two. He didn't waste any time. He got down on one knee and spoke words I can't remember. And I said, 'Yes!'

The moment seemed to flash by; the only thing that mattered was these 22-year-olds were engaged. We had mince, carrots and rice for dinner. Not the most romantic meal, but it was prepared with love and excitement by Brenden's sister. I knew well how tight the budget was. He has since made it up to me with many sumptuous dinners and holidays on gorgeous islands.

As my fiancé, he spent Christmas with my family for the first time, and it was a blissful fairy tale – one of the best Christmas holidays of my life.

Are you wondering about the wedding budget? Remember the size of my family – my mom's four siblings, my dad's crowd of brothers and sisters. Not to mention all the aunts and uncles on both sides of my mom's family with whom she is close, and the many friends my dad invites to everything he does. Brenden's family is not as big, so that was a relief, until his mom mentioned inviting their entire church.

Without flinching, we announced, 'Sorry, but we're only having 50 guests. And everybody must be dressed in black.'

There were objections. My mother-in-law said black was for funerals. But I was not willing to go into debt for a wedding, and eventually my mother-in-law was persuaded that black was actually very elegant. It looks better in the photographs, too. Even with my one aunt who decided to wear white – yes, bridal white. She felt completely out of place and a tittle embarrassed. (My family gets how particular – some might even say pedantic – I am about certain things. They have learnt to respect that.)

As for my dress, after searching high and low I finally found the perfect one at YDE for R900: golden-beige with delicate lace detailing. (A few months later, I saw pictures of a wedding where all the bridesmaids were wearing *my* dress; it kind of sucked, but by then Brenden and I were happily married and debt-free.)

The day the cows were brought we got married. I was determined to go home as Mrs Ledwaba, regardless of whether they reached an agreement or not. No one could convince me otherwise.

On our day, 14 January, we began with the beautiful lobola

ceremony, in the early morning. It was followed by a traditional lunch of mogodu and pap, a hit with everyone but Uncle Jack, Nonto and me. We didn't have a wedding cake; we simply forgot about it. The food was good and there was malva pudding instead.

My friend Althea had done my makeup. My aunt Boocy had taken me to a salon, where I got the best straight-back braids done, simple but beautiful. But my nails looked awful, as the ombré effect I'd asked for had turned into a lumpy pink mess. Brenden wore a blue suit that he found on sale at Zara, with a tie that his dad gifted him. Everybody complied with our attire request except my mother's aunt, who dressed in white. My best teenage friend Shooder was a bridesmaid, alongside my little sister, both also in black.

The photographer forgot to charge his camera and wasted most of his battery taking pictures outside. By the time my dad and I were ready to walk in, he told us to hurry up because the battery was dying. And all our pictures are blurry.

Because of an upset stomach, I was very bloated for most of the day. Was I sure I was getting married for love, or was I pregnant, my mother asked? (The bloating confused me as well.) My stomach eventually settled at around 6 pm, just in time for our wedding celebration, which took place at a guesthouse not far from my parents' home. My friend Dee was our MC.

That night, my new husband and I had a big fight. I was hell-bent on spending our first night at the guesthouse, but he had to get to his church job the next morning. so we got over it, packed our bags and headed back to Jozi. We spent our honeymoon in our new flat.

It wasn't the romantic wedding night I had hoped for but I went to bed Mrs Ledwaba.

REFLECTION

In this day and age of rehearsal dinners, a bunch of bridesmaids in matching pyjamas, a traditional and a white wedding with hundreds of guests, and making sure it's all Instagrammable, it's easy to forget what the joining of two people in holy matrimony is all about.

- If you are married, did your wedding match your expectations?
- What was your favourite part of it?
- What really didn't work for you (if anything)?
- What do you wish you had done differently?
- Write it all down.

If your wedding felt like it missed all the important stuff, the good news is you can always be like me and do it again. Although we got married in 2017, we had a traditional wedding in 2021, planned by my family. If you don't want to have a second wedding, there's always the opportunity to have a vow-renewal ceremony.

So remember, it's never too late to have your dream wedding!

You can't google cows

15

Growing pains

About a week after the wedding, my parents were eager to visit us at our new flat. However, we didn't have money to offer them anything, not even Tennis biscuits. I excitedly shared the news of their visit with my new husband. Who blatantly refused. In my immaturity, I argued, 'But my dad will buy the biscuits and tea.' And I watched Brenden's ego explode. That was one of our first big fights. I found myself catastrophising, imagining a future where my marriage would separate me from my family. But when Brenden said no, he meant business; I didn't push him any further. It's one of the funniest stories to tell these days, but it wasn't amusing then.

Our first year of marriage showed me who I do not want to be. When triggered or angered by him, I would sometimes shout like a madwoman, and occasionally jump in my car and drive away.

I finally realised that the person I used to be is not the person I aspire to become. About two years into the marriage, I decided that I would never raise my voice to anyone again, especially my husband. I find it extremely disrespectful. Perhaps a part of me felt this way when my mother apologised to my siblings and me for shouting at us a lot. (She, too, has evolved.)

These days I may have slipped up once or twice, but for the most part I've stuck to my commitment.

I remember a time when I cooked, cleaned the house and did laundry every day; it was during the first three to six months of our marriage. It wasn't expected of me, but I didn't have much going on besides studying for my beauty diploma, and I thought that's what a wife was supposed to do.

Boy, was I wrong, and I am glad of it. Not wrong about doing those things, but about limiting a woman's role to domestic chores. If such a role is what we value over everything else, how can we ever discover God's plan for us? It certainly helped that my husband barely noticed the lack of dust behind the washing machine or the twice-weekly fresh bedding. This irked me, and I found other things on which to focus my perfectionism – things that would at least make me money.

Our early days of marriage were fun and somewhat naive. We took on the traditional roles of husband and wife. I gave up more of myself than I would've wanted to, while my husband did not. It was my job, as I saw it, to make his dreams come true and to allow the aim of my existence to be led by him. I was deeply disappointed when I realised that he didn't see things that way, but the life we would create together would be ideal.

My expectations of marriage were high, and they felt like a page from a magazine that we just had to copy and paste into our lives. Trying to fit into traditional marriage norms caused a lot of friction, and neither of us felt fulfilled until we decided, 'Heck, let's do this our way.'

Growing up, the only birthday gift I could count on was the R20 note I got from my grandmother, Agnes. My mother would always make my favourite meal: her famous lasagne, or grilled chicken as I got older. But I rarely received birthday presents, until I met Brenden.

While gifts are not my primary love language, I look forward to his gifts, which are always paired with an experience. On the morning of my 27th birthday, I woke up to the sounds of Anita Baker. A saxophonist playing live in my living room was enough to bring me to tears, but it didn't end there. It was followed by an outfit for the day that he selected and bought for me, accompanied by a new Dior perfume, which I am still holding on to. We then had breakfast at a scenic restaurant in Houghton, one of my favourite suburbs because of its large trees spreading their branches over the streets. Brenden also gifted me my first designer item. We ended the day at a beautiful tree house, savouring chicken wings. It doesn't get more perfect than that. Each birthday I've spent with him has been special, but that one tops them all.

During our first year of marriage, having dropped out of my degree, being a musician felt like the only tangible thing that God could use me for. My idea of ministry was still limited to being either a worship singer or a pastor, and the latter was not part of the plan. I kept looking for ways to assist God in fulfilling His promise, and it became an obsession. Obsession often leads to manipulation and jealousy but, really, the root of it is fear.

At the time, Brenden was singing at a local church, for which he was getting paid well. He didn't have to work there during the week, which allowed him time to build his career. The money covered costs such as the rent and the car but wasn't enough for other things. I figured, if we could both be on the worship team, we would bring in double and all our life problems would be solved. I planned extensively, I prayed intensely and … it just didn't happen.

I was jealous and resentful of my husband. I envied his clarity about his calling, his ability to pursue it and his ability to earn from it. I felt it was unfair. These feelings consumed me until finally I accepted that it was not going to happen.

That Sunday rehearsal, when they welcomed the new girl, I knew it was time to let go. When I got home, I went to the spare bedroom and knelt down next to the pink velvet couch my grandmother had given us.

I cried out to God: 'I surrender.'

I asked God to take away my feelings of desire and to help me stop idolising the idea of serving Him. I released all my emotions by writing them in the new journal Brenden had given me for my birthday. I released not only my negative thoughts but also the dream I had held on to for a long time. I accepted being where I was in my life, I showed gratitude and I let go. And thereby banished my fear.

In that moment of letting go, I freed myself from living a life of limitation. Brenden saw my desperation; he even tried to help me get a job without compromising his place in the church, but it was an unfair expectation from my end. He never judged me for it; he understood. I idealise the idea of serving God. But once it became about having a relationship with Him rather than about what I could do for Him, my life changed. I became open to whichever way He wanted to use me.

I am still on that path, and He continues to put new desires in my heart. Things I would never have imagined.

While I was still finding my feet, our early years were filled with people asking Brenden, 'Aren't you the guy who was on *Idols*?

You should have won!' Each time, I witnessed him reliving the most humiliating and dream-crushing moment of his life, and we could do nothing but smile and agree.

I know people meant no harm, but it was extremely challenging for him. As a boy from a small village in Graskop, it was supposed to have changed his life. Spending most of his teenage years preparing for the competition, he had bet his life on winning it. While runner-up may sound like a dream for some, for him it diminished his light, and he slowly lost faith in God. He didn't become an atheist, but I could see that he was Christian by expectation only – his heart was too broken for him to continue fully believing.

Having completed my beauty course, I began to see clients at home. I was also working for my dad most weekdays. Brenden worked most weekends. On Mondays, we would drive to Cresta Mall, and go to a small restaurant that had a Monday special. We went not for the food but for the Wi-Fi, and, in my case, for a sense of purpose. It was at that restaurant that I started to dream outside of the box, doing research online and watching videos by incredible nail technicians. Brenden would download our weekly sermon. It was Pastor Steven Furtick who kept him going.

REFLECTION

Not every dream we have is going to come true. Sometimes they are stepping stones to something else. Sometimes they come true in different ways years later. Sometimes we realise that what we thought we wanted so badly actually isn't for us. On Brenden's first gospel album, he featured me in two songs. It was an incredible gift and the perfect way for an old dream to finally come to fruition, just not in the way I thought it would. A full-circle moment, indeed.

Now we are planning worship nights together, with all our gifts in full force and service. No limits.

Think of your dreams ...
- Have you ever had a dream that didn't work out?
- How did that make you feel?
- Did letting it go make space for what you really needed to do with your life?
- Write it all down.

Perhaps what you're meant to do is still coming. It could be that it wasn't a no but a not yet!

16

The good wife

For some, the idea of a woman being a good wife involves her keeping the house clean, preparing hot meals for her family and having a successful career. Guided by the examples set by my mother and grandmother, I have always seen a good wife as one who is educated, has a thriving career and runs a tight ship at home. Although I didn't finish my degree, I knew I was smart and an entrepreneur at heart.

After a long day of classes, Dee and I would daydream about a life without the burdens of studying. We would talk about our ideal careers, and our ideal marriages. In mine, my husband and I would have sex seven times a week, each day helped along by a different chapter of the *Kama Sutra*.

Go ahead and laugh; I had no idea.

In my and Brenden's first year of marriage, I took pride in starting my days early in prayer and a sermon from the Trinity Broadcasting Network, followed by study, research or hours of work, then rushing back home to clean, do laundry and whip up a Pinterest-inspired meal. And because our careers weren't thriving, we did have more time and energy for sex. I was always ready to be dessert, even though sometimes I was almost asleep by 8.30 pm.

A good wife was productive and independent, I thought, and that was exactly who I was going to be, even if it killed me. Gaining weight or getting out of shape was never an option. I would be the physically fit, petite wife with my nails up to date and my hair always on point.

MaNdlovu would wake up at 4 am to clean her yard, and while her home didn't have much, she took care of it as though it was situated in the smartest of suburbs. 'A girl wakes up before the sun is out. The sun should not be hitting your buttocks!' she would tell my female cousins and me. For most Zulu mothers, waking up any time after six was considered lazy and disgusting.

My mother also abhorred the idea of sleeping in when the home was messy. In her view, you wake up early, bathe and clean the house from top to bottom, and then you can go take a nap. Not me: I kept going until nightfall, and enjoyed it.

This waking-early lesson helped make me a person who takes care of herself and her space. However, I have had to unlearn the idea that rest is bad. In fact, rest is just as important as being active. In contrast to my hyper-productive personality, my husband is very laid-back. Growing up having no chores or responsibilities, he learnt how to cook only when I was pregnant and Mrs Crazy Hormones came stomping in!

By 24, it was becoming clear what kind of wife I would be. Brenden having been my friend before he became my husband really helped. As I started being honest about the unrealistic expectations I had created for myself, his empathy was clear. 'Babe, I married you for you, not what you do,' he told me.

Although I have hung up the mop and apron, I still consider productivity to be a trait of a good wife. I've simply shifted my efforts to different areas of my life. And as our family has grown and the demands of our careers have increased – as life in general has kept happening – our libidos have dipped. Sex seven times a week would be a stretch for us, and that's okay. There are many other ways to be intimate, as we would discover.

All you married women can stop laughing now.

Slowly I began unlearning, and finding out about myself. What a messy and beautiful road it is. I am not a 'good' or a 'traditional' wife, and my husband loves that about me. It's liberating – I no longer have to explain myself to anybody. And I confirm that as my journey unfolds, certain ideas will change or stay the same; either way, right now, they are true to me.

(Some things will never change, though: taking a shower or bath before bed, wearing perfume and sleeping in white linen!)

REFLECTION

These days, we have all kinds of expectations of ourselves (fuelled in no small way by social media). Have you got caught in the trap of thinking that a relationship needs to operate in a certain way? That you each need to assume a specific role for it to be a good, healthy relationship? It's well known that unhappiness is caused by the gap between the way we want things to be and the way they are.

- What did you think it meant to be a good wife or partner when you were growing up?
- How has the reality of being in a marriage or stable relationship changed your ideas about this?

- How do you feel about that reality? Do you feel like you are both fulfilling your life's purpose, or do you feel as though just one person in the relationship has the space to do that?
- Write it all down. And then go and scream into a pillow, if you need to!

The good wife

17

'My foot grew'

None of my pregnancies was planned; I'm just extremely fertile, and Brenden's pull-out game is hit-and-miss.

The day I found out I was pregnant, everything about that morning was normal. I woke up at the usual time and went for a session with my personal trainer. Despite the exercise, I noticed my body was changing, and not in a good way. I pushed myself as usual, and just as the session ended I vomited.

I knew that I might be pregnant. As I walked out of the gym, I immediately called my sister-in-law and my mother to tell them about the vomiting; both sent me to get a pregnancy test. It didn't take long to confirm that I was pregnant. In our room, Brenden and I knelt on the floor in awe of the life that was growing inside me. From that moment, everything changed.

Girl, I would love to tell you how miraculous my pregnancy felt, how I glowed and looked amazing, but I would be lying and this is not Instagram.

My pregnancy was messy and ugly. I mean UGLY. B.C, before children, I had perfect, perky 32C breasts and after finding out I was pregnant, my breasts took a dramatic turn south. I went straight to a saggy DD while the rest of my body seemed to be saying, 'Nah, we will catch up later.' Nausea tormented me every single morning, every car ride and every evening. The smell of acetone at my salon sent me straight to the toilet. All I wanted to do was sleep, eat and count the days till my due date.

No one suggested that I take my wedding ring off, so it was stuck until my swollen fingers went back to normal. And my feet! They grew from size 4 to 8, then down to 6. (I would've preferred 4, thank you very much.) My nose also expanded. My eyes and teeth felt like they were shrinking to give my nose more room. As I write this, it does sound a little funny, but at the time it was devastating.

It was a shock to the system, for me and my husband, even though he didn't say it. And not only him. One afternoon, even before greeting me, my grandmother said, 'Ah, my poor girl, what has this baby done to your face? I am sure it's a boy.' That's a funny thing about old people – they become children again and express themselves openly, while we hold everything in like a phlegmy cough in a quiet exam room. It's better to let it out. With love, of course. I giggled to try to make everyone a little more comfortable with my disfigured features and pigmentation, and in every similar moment I would smile and say, 'At least the baby is healthy.'

That was 24-year-old me; I am a whole different woman now.

Almost 20 kg down.

I was at the peak of fitness. The baby weight was gone, and I ran 5 km in less than 30 minutes with ease. Nuri was almost a year old, healthy and smart and with a good sleeping routine. Our marriage was finding its rhythm again. Everything was, dare I say, perfect.

Our first international trip was coming up; we were going to London.

I should have known something was off when Brenden jumped out of bed and I was too tired to join him. After about three days of struggling with what I thought was jet lag, I started to worry. I woke up ready to go to see my doctor, just to make sure I hadn't caught something on our trip. Stepping into the shower, a sudden thought struck me: maybe I should take a pregnancy test.

Once again, within a second it was positive.

My pregnancy with Zani was much easier. (Just as I had known Nuri would be a girl, I knew this new baby was a boy.) He let me keep my face, I had far less nausea and, with lockdown in full effect, I got to slow down, luxuriate in big T-shirts and tracksuits, and prepare little Nuri for the arrival of her brother. By three months, Zani was sleep-trained and eating solids. Both my babies were settling down well. As usual, I was eager to get back to work. I hosted an online conference, and started working out, regaining my pre-pregnancy body. I transitioned to a vegan lifestyle and began collaborating with various lifestyle brands. Everything was moving so fast and so thrillingly, I took barely a moment to breathe.

I noticed that I was getting flu every month and seemed very run-down. I attributed it to Nuri bringing germs home from crèche, but in retrospect I realise I was burnt out. I came to understand that I was working for validation. I wanted to be a picture-perfect, Instagrammable young mother with a thriving business and happy children. I would get sick, dose myself with medicine, pick myself up and carry on.

That was until I found out I was pregnant with baby number three.

Brenden named her Rose.

I couldn't connect. I felt only relief. I kept waiting for the day it would hit me and I would feel something else, but nothing has changed. I tried to shame myself into guilt and grief, but it didn't work, so I chose to give myself the grace of honesty. Let me explain …

Zani was a few months shy of a year old. With two babies under the age of two, I knew I was done having children. At least at that time. Emotionally, mentally and physically, I was exhausted, and I wanted to start feeling like myself again. My gynaecologist and I went through contraceptive options. I had fallen pregnant twice while on the pill; the injection made me bloated, the patch sent me into major depressive episodes. Just an IUD remained. The insertion procedure was lengthy and difficult because of my inverted uterus, but once it was done, everything felt normal, and our libidos were back in sync.

Two months later, my period had not visited me and I immediately knew that something was wrong.

Brenden went to get the pregnancy test. And again, the result was positive.

'I can't handle another baby,' I sobbed. 'I can't do it, I just can't.'

Brenden was empathetic, but he didn't see it as the upheaval I was experiencing. For him, whether planned or not, a baby is a blessing. With the first two babies, I felt the same way. This time it was different.

I called my mother in tears. 'It's okay to be sad now, but soon you will accept it. Once the baby's here, you'll be happy,' she told me.

'No, Mama, I will not. I can't keep popping babies out. I am tired. My body is tired. I am content with the two that I have. I want to get back to being me.'

I spent the entire weekend in bed, crying. I also spent a lot of time readings blogs of moms with three children under three. None of them reassured me. The pictures were cute, and the I-eventually-loved-it stories were touching, but I just couldn't see myself in that situation.

Furious that yet another contraceptive device had failed me, I dragged myself to my gynae. She immediately picked up that the baby was growing in the wrong place – in one of my fallopian tubes. I didn't fully understand what that meant. Was it dangerous? What was going to happen now? The doctor informed us that we needed to terminate the pregnancy to prevent a potentially fatal rupture of the tube. I wish I could say I was devastated to hear that, but all I felt was relief that I didn't have to carry the baby to term.

I took a pill to terminate the pregnancy. That weekend my parents came to see me and the children. Brenden left for work in another province, and my dad went to a birthday party he was invited to. So it was my mother, my two children and me. I'd been told to expect some discomfort.

It began with a sharp pain, almost like a period cramp. It was a Sunday evening, and my doctor was away. My tolerance for pain being quite high, I could manage, I told myself. A few moments later the intensity shot up to a 12 out of 10. *Discomfort?* No, this was life or death. Bonolo rushed me to hospital while my mom stayed at home to look after Nuri and Zani. On the phone, I told Brenden I was going to die. The pain was so bad that I started vomiting.

I went into casualty in agony, and came out with no baby. I was as sick as a dog and confused as hell, but I was also eased. I knew that if I had another baby, one of us would suffer. Either I was going to die inside, or the baby was going to be neglected and would grow up knowing it was unwanted. I wasn't being dramatic.

I've seen mothers raise children for whom they had no emotional capacity, and I know that I was headed in that direction as well. Antenatal depression – in fact, mental health in general – is not taken as seriously as it should be in our community. Coming from a family with a history of alcoholism, addiction, bipolar disorder and mental health issues, I have witnessed the long-term effects of ignoring such conditions.

We lost my cousin Amy to suicide; after multiple attempts, she succumbed to the rope that cut her breath short at my grandmother's house. She had been hospitalised in September 2019, was put on antidepressants and then discharged. We spent that December together. She appeared happy and well, sounding stronger and even thanking me for the journal I'd bought her. We presumed that she would be all right. This was because we knew so little about mental illness, how it doesn't just 'get better' like the flu. But in January 2020, Amy lost the fight.

This experience opened my eyes and prompted me to be the first one in my family to go to therapy. I was lucky that I wasn't left with any permanent scarring from the ectopic pregnancy but I was left with emotional damage.

Following this pregnancy, I never went on any more contraceptives. But if I got a headache, I took a pregnancy test. If I felt dizzy at the gym, I took a test. Anything remotely related to being pregnant, I took a test.

Emotionally, I was a mess, and had to deal with ongoing comments on social media such as 'Are you pregnant?', 'We see a bump', 'Somebody is getting chubby'. All I could do was move on as though I was not bothered. Every comment a woman could get about her body, I got, while silently dealing with what had happened. My hormones were equally in turmoil, my body continuing to 'be pregnant' long after the baby was gone. I lost my body for some time, and regaining ownership of it has been a lengthy battle.

I often think about my grandparents living in the home where we lost Amy. In their generation, therapy was not seen as a solution. But time by itself, I believe, does not heal all wounds. It is the combination of time and the processing of pain that better equips us to handle grief and loss. I went back to therapy full-time, by myself and with Brenden. He needed it as well.

Mental health is a battle unseen but is as real as the physical pain we are hospitalised for.

REFLECTION

It's tempting to have airbrushed ideas of what becoming a mother is all about. But as with mental health issues, the matter is not as simple as we would like it to be.

Think of your own pregnancy-related experience(s) …

- Did you find it easy to get pregnant, or was it a struggle? Did you have to undergo fertility treatment?
- Did you experience a miscarriage? How did you feel about it?
- Maybe you decided not to have children, or perhaps you wanted children but were unable to conceive. What comments have you had to put up with as a result of this?
- When you were pregnant, did you suffer from depression? Did your feet also grow? Did you get piles, heartburn, stretch-marks and saggy boobs?
- Make a list of everything you had to let go of (including sleep!) after becoming a mother, and allow yourself a pity party for those perfect boobs you once had.

'My foot grew'

18

Some things fall apart

So often, when things seem to be coming together in one part of your life, they fall apart in another. Brenden's and my careers were thriving, but thorns in our rosebush began to prick us.

In March 2023, just after the Unlimited Fest, we were fulfilled but tired. It took so much out of us, in many respects.

I've always loved bringing people together, from hosting Christmas to connecting friends or a mentor and mentee. Uniting people and building communities. The first event I did was Hello Gorgeous. Mahalia and I brought 200 women together at the World of Yamaha Theatre in Sandton, coalescing music, people and conversations. Then I opened my salon and, every month, we would have gatherings of 15 to 20 ladies. When my YouTube channel started growing, the more 'unpopular' things – such as conversations about purpose, marriage, career and motherhood – had a real impact. Slowly I started to understand my gift and ability to create safe spaces for people to have difficult conversations.

In 2020, three months after Zani was born, I hosted an online event that took place over three days and streamed it live for free. I gathered singer Shekhina, Mogau Seshoene (The Lazy Makoti) and personal-finance coach Mapalo Makhu and we pre-recorded conversations on finances, life purposes and careers in podcast-interview style (before I even knew what a podcast was). We created a poster and live-streamed it throughout a long weekend. More than 1 000 people from all over Africa tuned in at the same time. That's when I knew that there was a market for my work. When the country started opening up, I held a Pilates event, bringing together about 100 people. While the exercise was exciting, it was the conversations and speaking element that stood out.

At the beginning of 2022, I decided to organise an event with the aim of creating an environment from which every attendee would leave feeling empowered to achieve anything they set their mind to.

In March 2023 we held the first Unlimited Fest.

I had no idea that the 'unlimited' would stick. It was just a theme. But then again that's how most of my ideas start – as a 'by the way' thought or an add-on in passing – and as I continue to honour the small moments or ideas by bringing them to life, they become big ideas.

Our first event was a major success and gave us some tough lessons. Women from Zambia, Zimbabwe, Botswana, Eswatini and all parts of South Africa attended. And the energy was insane. We cried, we laughed and we danced in a life-changing experience. I didn't know what it would become but knew that I had done what God had asked of me.

Earlier that year, on 12 January, I woke up expecting the best from the day, as usual. I might have been a little more excited that week: it was two days before our wedding anniversary, and I had planned a short getaway. My parents were coming to town, and the ladies at the office were doing well. It was about two months to the festival, and all our plans were coming to fruition. I'd been working out and was in great shape. Brenden filmed me leaving the house. I wore a brown crop top, black Paige jeans that I got in New York and a cute block semi-heel, and carried my Fendi tote on the left and my car keys on the right. Just for the video, I popped on my sunglasses. (I love collecting sunglasses, though seldom wear them.)

Starting my fairly new car, I realised that it was low on petrol. I was late for an appointment with my skin aesthetician and convinced myself I would make it – I had done it before. You don't think something like this will ever happen to you until it does. About five minutes from my destination, my car began to slow down on a steep rise; then, in the middle of traffic, it stopped. Other cars sped by, the drivers noticing me only as they came dangerously closer. I called Brenden. Frustrated as he was, because of the number of times he had warned me about this very situation, he agreed to come and get me.

Despite the heat and discomfort, I kept my seatbelt on, just moving my seat back while waiting for him. I cancelled my appointment, and then called Nonto. While deep in conversation with my younger sister, I heard a loud bang.

My phone dropped, my eyes snapped shut. The next moment, my car was on the paving in the middle of the road. My sister heard it all. She immediately called back. I reassured her that physically I was all right. But the shock was too much.

As I stepped out of my car, I realised that if I hadn't kept my seatbelt on and adjusted my seat back, my face would have been smashed or I would have gone through the windscreen. The impact was serious. The lady who had crashed into me from behind had been driving extremely fast and talking on her phone. Neither of us was hurt, but both our cars were written off.

Brenden and I spent hours at the police station while, shaking with shock, I gave my statement; we then went to casualty for me to have internal checks and finally returned home to some comfort food. I slept for the rest of the day.

Being so busy, I found it difficult to pay attention to my emotions. With Fest just a month away, I immediately plunged back into my routine, knowing we had planned a trip to Bali, which would be my opportunity to relax and rejuvenate.

Bali was one of the most incredible experiences of our lives. Getaways in general bring Brenden and me closer, but this one was different. It seemed as though God was reaffirming His plans for our life as a couple; the trip felt purposeful, sexy, fun, exciting and wild. We got to enjoy each other and remember the parts that parenthood tends to obscure. On our last day we lay in bed, with rain sliding across the window blurring the view of the gorgeous greenery outside, and we opened our hearts to each other. We made plans, to be followed by action steps as soon as we got home. We were excited!

At the airport, we rushed to upgrade our flights, as we normally do. There was only one business class seat left.

'It's fine, we'll leave it,' I said.

But Brenden insisted. 'I want you to rest. I promise I will be fine.'

In that moment, I remembered that he has always sacrificed for me, throughout our lives together.

We agreed that we would order food to be delivered as soon as we landed, and I would cook pap. But life had other plans.

Arriving home, I was puzzled to see water trickling down the driveway. As I opened our front door, out poured a river, gushing down from upstairs. It took a moment for us to realise that our home had flooded. And while we were trying to process this, our chicken dinner arrived.

I ran upstairs to find that the tap of the bath in the children's bathroom had been left open and the plug in place. My mother and our helper had stayed at our house for three days, then gone to my mom's until we were back – about seven days in total. On the day that they left, our area was without water. Opening the tap to find nothing coming out, they skipped bathing the children and left for Middelburg.

At some point the water in our area was turned back on. It filled the bathtub to the brim, overflowed, then ran through the children's bedrooms and down the stairs, streaming into every room on the ground floor, damaging the walls, drowning the floors. The food in the fridge and freezer rotted because the water caused the electricity to short. Our bedroom and Brenden's studio were the only rooms to survive. Did I mention that we had just added wooden floors and done some renovations to our home? Funnily enough, we had decided to take a break from doing more work in the house to give us some time to enjoy it.

The water had been running for a week when I closed the tap. And it felt like I closed the tap of joy in our lives, at least for a while.

As you can imagine, the smell was horrible. The stench from the meat and vegetables in the warm fridge mixed with the rotting wooden floors was so powerful that flies filled the house and started crawling on our food. My Chicken Licken consumption decreased greatly after that!

Responding to our call, our construction team cleaned up as

best as they could. The first night, we went to rest at my parents' house. Brenden feels all his emotions in real time, and if that means taking a break he will do so. I, on the other hand, go into problem-solving mode. We've always known and understood that about each other, but this was too much.

Slowly but surely, we shifted from being in this together to fighting about how to deal with the situation. We became each other's enemy.

REFLECTION

Let's face it, it's easy to be nice to our partner when things are going well. You're both earning money, you have a nice house, you get on with each other's families. But what happens when things aren't going so well? If one of you gets retrenched, or you're in debt, or there's illness or a bereavement to cope with? What happens when life happens?

Think back to difficult situations you've experienced as a couple ...
- How did you handle them?
- How did your partner handle them?
- Did these situations bring you together or drive you apart?
- Do you wish you or your partner had handled things differently? How?
- Write it all down.

19

The seven-year itch

You may not know about the seven-year itch until you're in it ...
google it and you'll see what I mean. What I'm not sure of is
whether it's during year six going on seven or during year seven
going on eight. But what I can tell you is that it is absolute hell.

As I've always shared, I don't believe in labelling a year a 'good'
one or a 'bad' one. I always ride the wave, take the lessons, enjoy
the good times and maintain faith or an optimistic attitude during
the bad. I believe you can't control what happens to you – all
you can control is how you respond to it. Then 2023 happened.
Experiencing stress in your career and other life matters is bad
enough, but if not seeing eye to eye with your spouse and trying
to argue in whispers so as not to upset the children is added,
then it is much worse. I don't know exactly when the bickering
started, but I would choose it over the silent treatment and one-
word answers.

We were both focused on big projects: I was working on my
first Unlimited Fest, Brenden was producing one of the biggest

albums to come out that year. We fully backed each other up, as we always do, and in theory understood the necessary sacrifices.

After having survived the car accident and losing my car, holding a successful festival with over 1 000 attendees and releasing two successful albums, we needed to slow down and spend quality time together. And we did. That's what Bali was about. We felt connected to each other again; we found a new rhythm, a new attraction and an excitement to grow closer and nurture our family. But as soon as we landed in South Africa and stepped into our waterlogged home, things began to slip away. Everything we had fought through and worked through was destroyed.

Fresh from Bali, our attitude was that we would conquer this problem together. Then Monday came, and on Mondays the over-achiever in me always kicks in. In a crisis, I go into super-fixer mode. My husband, on the other hand, sleeps his feelings away.

During hard times we both withdraw; we just do it differently. I look for something to keep me busy – a new problem to solve, a new box to tick, a mission to prove how strong I am at whatever cost. Brenden goes to bed.

While he felt his feelings and pain in real time, I tried to cover mine with optimism and gratitude. And the wedge started growing. Every day was war and a painful reminder that we had to put our new plans on hold.

To dry the house out, we had to keep the windows open. We slept in one room, children and all, and had one room to cook in. As the temperature dropped each night, our hearts towards each other grew colder; we were now on different teams. My resentment increased as I felt that I was the only one fixing the mess, while Brenden napped or complained. Brenden grew angrier at the fact that I was trying to cover the trauma and pain we had just experienced with toxic positivity.

We were right to express ourselves in the ways we know how to, and wrong to judge the other.

Not only was our physical home destroyed, but it felt as though the foundation of our marriage was cracking. One day I woke up and asked myself if I had made a mistake. I even texted my mother: 'I don't think I should be married.' It was the Easter weekend, and we had committed to being back to church full-time after a sabbatical during lockdown. Our church had a conference that weekend and we were excited! The morning of Good Friday was the first time I finally cracked and acknowledged the severity of what had happened to our home. I called my sister-in-law, packed our bags and drove there. She and her husband got us to sit down and talk – well, more venting than talking, but at least we laughed. This was one of the easier days of 2023.

If I had to provide the details of every fight, you would probably be shocked at the eventual outcome. We exchanged words that should never have left our mouths. We threw tantrums and argued in front of the children. We got to a point where each of us chose ourselves and our conversations were reduced to who would drop off the kids and who would buy bread. I was watching my marriage slip away, and felt powerless to stop it. Brenden started searching for flats in the area we live in because we thought he should move out but it made sense for him to stay close to the children and work. It was then that I started to think that this was just a 'season' of marriage.

Some seasons are filled with excitement, and some are kept going by the responsibilities of raising children and paying bills. We had a podcast to do, and although Brenden committed to train a new team to produce it, we knew that that would be going against what God had instructed us if he quit. So, we kept the podcast going, and it kept us together.

Having booked our family holiday at the beginning of the year, as usual, we decided not to cancel our upcoming trip to Dubai. But when we left we were not talking again, except if it was about the kids. Until one night in the hotel, we found ourselves willing to put our egos aside.

Me: 'I think we should get a divorce.'

Brenden: 'I agree.'

Me: 'Can we commit to enjoying this holiday with the kids, and then focus on the next steps when we get home?'

Brenden: 'I'm in.'

And that's how we got our marriage back: we gave it up. When the idea of giving it up became real, we realised that was not what we wanted. In Dubai we got a clear picture of where we were and what we did want. And we've always wanted each other. From the age of 20 we've always had each other, carried each other, protected each other, hurt each other but ultimately forgiven each other. We have won together and lost together. We had given our everything to each other and to our family, and this was certainly not the end. I wish I could say, there was a magic wand that made everything good again, but we simply chose to work it out. It was lots of individual therapy and couples' therapy again, more sex and better conflict management.

There are days I wake up filled with gratitude and a sense of my marriage being God's plan. And there are days I wake up in hell. But we chose to stick out the seven-year itch, and we are still standing.

REFLECTION

No relationship is perfect. Every relationship is going to go through rough patches. Some will be like small potholes in the road, others will feel like a natural disaster that uproots the foundations. And you are the only one who gets to decide if standing in the rain is worth it.

Think about your own relationship ...
- Have you experienced the seven-year itch?
- What did you do to get your relationship back on track?
- This is a brilliant exercise to do from Imago therapy:
  - Let your partner tell you what they are upset about. Don't interrupt. When they are finished, you will reflect back what they said, which means you have to listen. (For those of us who are busy concocting our own arguments in our heads, this is not easy.) They can gently correct you if they think you got it wrong.
  - Then you acknowledge what they've been through and sincerely apologise for the hurt they've experienced.
  - The next day, or week or weekend, it's your turn to speak and your partner's turn to listen and reflect back.
- Write it all down.

PART THREE
The cost of
the calling

20

Trolls, stalkers and friendships

31 January 2024, a Wednesday morning.

I woke up at 5 am, walked downstairs, grabbed my water and prayed while making my way to my office. Through the window the sky was darker than usual for that time of year. It was a big day. I had one of the most important podcasts of my career. I was going to interview Cassper Nyovest, the biggest hip-hop star in South Africa.

As I usually do, I asked the Holy Spirit to give me the courage, the strength and the words. Then I sat down to start writing. (The first hour of my day is occupied with writing and praying.)

But I also did what I tell everybody not to do: I opened my phone and went on Twitter.

Out of nowhere, a smear campaign was going on about me.

'She's a mean girl and hides behind Christianity.'

And: 'She uses Jesus to cover her meanness.'

It went on and on, and just when I thought I had seen enough, it went on some more.

The conversation revolved around my struggles to maintain lasting friendships, particularly in the public eye, identifying specific instances and concluding that it was my fault.

My fault that all six or seven of us were no longer friends.

My first thought was 'How can people be so mean?'

Let me rephrase that: 'How can black women be so mean to other black women?'

A woman I don't know made it her mission for the day to gather people to discuss what a mean, fake and controlling person I am. And I didn't get to respond or defend myself. Hard as it is, you never wrestle with pigs, as you both get dirty.

In those moments, my body trembled from the sting of the words. I have endured online bullying, I have gone to therapy and gathered tools to deal with it and, most importantly, I know that I need to believe the truth of God's word about me, but the pain caused by those words lives on in my heart.

I got dressed, laced up my shoes, went for a walk and listened to a sermon. Bearing in mind the importance of not running away from my feelings, I allowed the anger, the pain and the fear of being disliked to flow through me. My heart swelled with toxic liquid and the back of my neck stung as I realised all the emotions and words that were not true about me.

I returned home to help my children get ready for school, and I prayed some more. What happened next is something that I've always known in my heart to be true. Coming upon John 15:16, I knew that God was real, and intentional about me.

'You have not chosen Me, but I have chosen you and I have appointed and placed and purposefully planted you, so that you would go and bear fruit and keep on bearing, and that your fruit will remain and be lasting, so that whatever you ask of the Father in My name [as My representative] He may give to you.'

Two things jumped off the page for me: He chose me just as I am. His approval of me was enough, and I had work to do.

Relief washed over me as I realised that those people had tried to discredit me and make me feel insecure, but God had stepped in and sent a direct message to me: 'Girl, I approve of you, and I did so before anything, or anyone.'

I wept while my children ran around screaming, waiting to go to school. Later, I told Brenden what had happened. I will never forget his response: 'So, you had some friendships that didn't work out? And that was, like, two years ago. So what? If that's all they can say about you, then let them.'

Now, fam, I don't claim to be perfect – always upbeat, always in the character. I have bad days, and moments of feeling sorry for myself. But I will never go out of my way to hurt anyone. I am quick to leave spaces that don't bring out the best in me, which is why my *public* friendships didn't work out. I wasn't going to write about the troll and the bullying, but that would be omitting a major part of my adult life. But the truth is that it hurts, and it unintentionally alters the way one interacts with people.

Going through the tweets again, I identified something: all of them had very little to do with me. People were upset that I have clear boundaries and am free to leave situations that no longer serve me, I run a business and I'm a woman – which, in their eyes, means I'm not confident, I'm bossy.

My public friendship fallouts created the perception that I can't keep friends, and the shame story was built around that. I was not willing to talk about what happened, to protect not only the other party but my work as well. Unfortunately, I didn't always receive the same courtesy, and only half the story was told. Here is how the situation transpired …

Inspired by my mother and her group of friends, I felt that I would love to have something like that: a group of friends with similar interests. Taking a deep breath, I identified seven wonderful ladies who, just like me, had married young and worked in the same or a similar industry, and I invited them to a 'sexy wives'-themed lunch. The theme related to our outfits, and was neither a group name nor implied a wives' club.

We had a time of laughter and vulnerability, and we enjoyed creating content around the lunch.

In my innocence, I thought sharing this would encourage people who may have felt alone, like me, to do the same. But it had the opposite effect: I started getting applications from people to join the 'sexy wives' club'. Everything moved so fast that while our relationships were brand new, we started getting offers from brands, the content grew our visibility and the pressure began to build. Pressure that was too much for a young friendship.

In our innocence and immaturity, our meet-ups became events and opportunities for content rather than for friendship and connection. While I made it my mission to show less of my private life as I was getting the online hate, for others, it was showing our experiences.

We did everything we could to save our friendship group, but some things are seasonal.

I still love those girls, my heart is happy when they do well and we have a good time when we see each other, but I could not sustain being part of the public friendship group. My goals don't allow me to, and I finally gave myself permission to say that even while people were judging me for it.

I don't make it to every baby shower, birthday, gathering or even family commitment. I used to cry myself to sleep about that, but it's the path that has chosen me. Brenden has always understood it, but I could never surrender to it. Perhaps it's because I've seen my mother nurture friendships for over 30 years. I've watched her show up for every funeral, every birthday party – you name it – and I held myself up to that standard. My dad showed up where he could, in making financial contributions and phone calls, but mostly had his head buried in his business. I don't think he felt bad – men are not expected to show up in that way. Like most of us, I set my standard of how I am meant to show up according to gender, rather than personality.

When my mother was offered career opportunities that would alter her life, she turned them down. She did this for various reasons, one of them being to be fully present, and I am confident that her decision gives her peace and joy. My dad finds joy in bigger and better, but misses out on some things.

I am a lot like my dad. I find fulfilment in reaching my highest potential. It comes at the cost of not being at every occasion, but I get to reach other women who, just like me, need permission to be themselves. Perhaps I couldn't sustain public friendships, but I have incredible friends who know and understand me and appreciate my privacy. We enjoy our relationships offline.

My husband has given me permission to be the ambitious woman I am, and he delights in it. I miss some moments, but in everything I do I am fully present and give my all. I would rather live in that honesty than live a half-hearted life where my boundaries are trampled over and I stay in relationships that don't work for my dreams. To the woman who sparked that Twitter conversation, you are probably hurting, and I get that, so I want to gift you with permission to be yourself. Not everyone will like it, but you will be free.

Just like any other relationship, not all friendships will last.

But, as I have found, in my gracefully letting go, God has been faithful in bringing the right people for me in this season.

Are you wondering about that podcast? At first I was shocked that Cassper even wanted to appear on it, and then I half-expected him to stand me up. But he didn't, and his enthusiasm and excitement for the podcast blew my mind. I thought that it would go viral, and it did. If you haven't seen it already, it is worth checking out, even if I say so myself.

REFLECTION

In the old days, gossip was something you might say about someone over a cup of tea or something stronger, or perhaps over the phone. That was bad enough, but now with social media gossip has gained the ability to ruin lives – tragically, even end them. This is something to consider, gal pal, before you next comment on or retweet or repost something about someone, even a celebrity – because they, too, are just people.

- Have you experienced hate – either in person or online – that's made you question who you are?
- How did you deal with it?
- Have you ever commented on, retweeted or reposted something and regretted having done that?
- Did you apologise?
- How do you wish you'd handled it, in retrospect?
- Write it down.

21

At what cost?

I think we don't speak enough about the cost of following our purpose. The Bible does, through the lives of Joseph, David, Naomi and Jesus himself – but we don't seem to do so.

I tend to doubt the real reason for everything I do; I minimise its value because I can't fathom the idea that, just maybe, what I do is as impactful and significant as what Joseph did in his time. And because I downplay the mission, I rationalise the storms I face by viewing them as coincidence rather than what they really amount to – a calling ordained by God.

Today, I asked myself: at what cost?

It's a question I have never asked myself before, but maybe it's never been as meaningful as it is right now. Meaningful in the sense that I come from generations of trauma.

I was about 20, committed to church, my studies, work and my relationship with Jesus, and I had just got out of a bed where I had been with a man I had no business being there with.

I was a committed Christian but I loved sex more, and so I would find myself fornicating on a Saturday night and then lifting my hands in worship on stage on a Sunday morning. I've always known that this was wrong, but I no longer believe that I was pretending on those Sunday mornings. I was genuinely doing both. Pretence is the heaviest burden some Christians carry, I believe.

Now, I wouldn't call myself a hypocrite (as I previously labelled myself); I just loved feeling wanted, but I also loved Jesus.

'Am I pretending to love God, or do I really love Him? If I really love Him, why do I do the things that I do?'

I've been there, and to be honest I still find myself there at times, knowing the truth but living in condemnation, which by the way has no power to change a person. Only an encounter with the love of God can do that.

On a chilly Saturday afternoon, I was at a choir workshop, excited to learn about how to serve the church more effectively and how to sing better (you know, the 'performance' part of things). I was saved, I had given my life to Christ at the age of 13 and I fully understood what I was doing. But I had not fully surrendered my will. As Pastor W began to speak, sitting pretty in my new red jacket my heart was beating so hard I could hear it. It felt like nothing I'd ever experienced before. I started weeping.

My spirit was at war with my flesh. Light and dark were wrestling for me, and all my physical form could do was sob and yearn to be freed. In front of my peers, I gave up my dignity for freedom. As the altar call came for those who wanted to be released from sexual bondage, I ran, hoping that others would join me so I wouldn't look and feel like the only one. I knew I wasn't alone, but I stood alone. Fearful, ashamed, everybody knowing my business, but light had won the war. I got home feeling liberated and ready to focus only on God.

But my habits and surroundings had not changed. I found

myself in bed with that man again, committed to Christ but scared and with no tools to fully escape the trap of sin and addiction. As soon as he left, I shed tears of disappointment, and it was at that moment that God anointed and appointed me. In the trap of sin, God told me that I would be the one to break generational curses in my family, that He had chosen me to do that.

'How? How can it be me? Do you not see what I just did? I am unreliable, I can't undo that.'

I heard His voice again: 'You will break generational curses.'

That was the last time I was in bed with this particular man; the calling was too great. It was not the last time I would be tempted, but it was the last time I gave in.

In my family there is alcoholism, poverty, multiple children outside of marriage, illness, sexual addiction and dysfunction. So when I heard 'break generational curses', I focused on not repeating the cycles of my family. It became clear to me that my calling in this world is to give permission to heal. It's in everything that I do – in my podcast, on social media, in my newsletters and events, and now in my book. I didn't think it would come at the cost of so much chaos, which is why I ask *at what cost*? What is the cost of breaking the generational trauma of someone I don't know through my own story? What is the cost of showing genuine empathy towards a stranger with a dying parent? What is the cost of holding an event not only with healing as its theme but with the manifestation of healing in all its aspects? What is the cost of the call? What is the cost of teaching faith?

Earlier in the day that I wrote this, I lay in a bath filled with bubbles in my beautiful bathroom lit by a scented candle, and once again I wept for the war within me. The war between light and darkness.

The difference is that now the darkness is giving up on the call to break generational trauma and curses, and the light is carrying a painful cross, which costs me everything but frees generations. And so I ask, at what cost?

Sometimes, it's having to be the boss, having to take unpopular decisions that are going to make you look like the bad guy and expose you to online hate, and sometimes you're going through a really rough time but you can't complain because everyone thinks your life is perfect.

I think about my teenage years, and realise that I always felt judged and that I would be caught out for being a fraud. By the age of 16 I was fully sexually active, not because I enjoyed it or had mind-blowing orgasms and relationships but because I was having a trauma response. If I initiated sex, I would never lose control of the situation again. Control became my weapon of protection.

I owe the younger Mpumi an apology for being so judgemental of and hard on her. I expected so much from her, I drowned her in a purity culture that had kicked her out without her permission. I compared her to made-up perfect girls who saved themselves for marriage, who had self-control, who didn't even think about sex. I didn't consider the violation of my little body; I didn't consider that somebody shoved me into that cycle of sexual disorientation.

I am glad that people have started talking openly about rape, molestation and sexual violation. But are we talking about the aftermath as well? We are not, and that's why the statistics of rape and molestation keep climbing. Rapists are not necessarily born rapists; most likely they are victims who have become villains – as we know, hurt people hurt people. If the healing work is never done, the cycle continues, whether forcefully or secretly, like mine. I want no young girl ever to experience the pain of secrecy and confusion that happens after sexual abuse, the pain of hiding how you respond to trauma because you don't have the tools to understand what happened to you.

REFLECTION

We have all been called to do something in this life, be it pursuing a career, caring for our children, helping out at church, singing in the choir, coaching our local sports team or, as in my case, sharing stories, being open and vulnerable so that others are given permission to heal.

- What is your calling? Don't think too much, just write it down. You might be surprised what comes out!
- What is the cost of your calling? Perhaps you cannot attend every sports match for your children because of your work, or perhaps you have chosen to be a stay-at-home parent and given up your career. Maybe you've chosen a career that entails working nights and public holidays. Maybe your income is inconsistent but you are doing work that you love and that is meaningful.
- Write it all down.
- Now make peace with everything that you've had to relinquish because it doesn't align with your calling.

At what cost?

22

Not once
but twice
or more

In 2008 I became intimately familiar with lack of control, loss and shame.

I had gained a place at the high school of my choice, which had one English class per grade and a brilliant sports and academic reputation; only 30 English – read black – children could be accepted.

On receiving my acceptance I knew that my future was in good hands, and my parents were proud. I had just grown my hair in a big, beautiful, soft Afro. My grey strands were starting to appear, and I was embracing it. The preceding December felt too long as I prepared for my new year in high school.

I showed up on my first day of school feeling beautiful, smart and chosen. I wore white socks, black school shoes from Woolworths, a crisp white short-sleeved shirt, a green pullover, and a green skirt that my mother had shortened for my petite body and bow legs. I immediately made friends; some from my previous primary school and some of whom I met on the day. As part of our induction and initiation, we were required to sit in a corner that was reserved for the Grade 8s. We were at that stage when girls start developing faster and boys our age looked awkward, all big noses that don't fit their faces, and lanky bodies, and some with acne. Our eyes were on the older boys. My crush seemed cute, innocent and out of reach; all the other girls found him cute too.

We went on camp. With our bags packed and buzzing with excitement, we jumped on the bus. Being in the minority, all the black children stuck together. At our campsite there was a dorm room for the guys and another for the girls. Each room had single beds that we could personalise for the weekend ahead. The bathroom facilities featured shared showers, but this wasn't an issue because most of the girls preferred to shower in the comfort of their own homes. For me, hygiene is right up there with breathing – I was going to be using the showers every night.

On our first day, I wore a brown Billabong boob tube with a pair of denim shorts. My perky breasts held up my top without the aid of a bra. I looked cute and I knew it. A group of friends and I chatted and laughed together outside while waiting for the programme to start. Then our group leaders began a game, chasing us with water balloons. I was a fast runner, so I took off and headed into a corner away from the crowd. He followed me. It was exciting and I liked it; I felt seen.

One moment I was running and laughing, the next moment I was rolling on the ground. I didn't get hurt, but my top slid off and out popped my perky yellow breasts. Embarrassed, I quickly pulled my top straight. I knew that, in that moment, in his eyes I was no longer just another Grade 8 learner but a beautiful young woman. I could see it. But, like a gentleman, he merely apologised and walked away.

We spent the weekend eyeing each other, knowing there was a line we couldn't cross. He was my leader and therefore off limits. I was 13 going on 14, he was a few years older. Writing my age all these years later feels shocking; I remember that at the time I felt grown-up but realise now just how young I was.

After camp, I looked forward to school every day, hoping to get a glimpse of my crush, at break, at athletics practice or in the corridors during class change. Every time I saw him, butterflies fluttered in my stomach. I knew he had a girlfriend, but who doesn't enjoy the thrill of a crush, especially at that age, when you don't even think about sex? A kiss, at most, no more than that.

On our way back from sports trips, we would take the bus. Those late-night journeys were known for mischief, for celebrating, singing, stopping to grab food and sitting with your girlfriend or boyfriend at the back, kissing. After a few of these trips, I found myself there, making out in the darkness.

'Is this really happening to me? Wow, I can't believe he chose me. He actually likes me!'

It gave me a thrill, and a sense of lust and achievement.

I had been kissed before but it became a lot more intense; hands were in places that had never been touched till then. It's normal, everyone in the bus was doing it, I told myself. But I was light-skinned, pretty, 14 and with the guy everybody wanted. The experience wasn't normal or acceptable; it was problematic. I became a rumour: I was the fast girl. But it didn't stop me from racing to the back on every bus ride.

I was never his girlfriend, he never asked me out, but the attraction was evident. He was kind when he knew that he could have a moment with me, but for the most part he ignored me. I was desperate for his attention.

Then MaNdlovu passed away.

I was away in Potchefstroom for a netball game. We had just won, the weather was amazing and everyone was laughing. My dad, who didn't believe in children having phones, had lent me his Motorola, which I would pretend was mine. I whipped out the phone to catch up with my older brother, Tough Guy, and kept calling until he answered. Eventually he picked up.

Me, jokingly: 'Have you spoken to Dad?'

Him, and I'll never forget this moment: 'Yes, I know, Gran died. We will talk later.'

I didn't know … I had no words. My grandmother had been ill for some time after suffering a stroke, but we didn't expect her not to make it. She had been living with us and sleeping in my bedroom. As she seemed to be recovering, she asked to go back to her home. I thought she was okay, but now she was gone. The rest of the day passed in a blur, and I found myself once again at the back of the bus on the way home.

MaNdlovu's funeral was at her home eCinci. Wanting to attend church the next morning, I got a lift home with my maternal grandparents and cousin, Pinks. We went to church, I in cream-coloured jeans, a brown knit jersey and my favourite boots. That afternoon, Pinks went to see her long-term boyfriend. Things felt different; after my grandmother's passing, my emotions were heightened. I texted him to let him know that I was home alone, not expecting a response (he never responded to my texts).

'I am on my way. Meet me halfway.'

I didn't even bother putting on decent underwear. I was 14, and the most that would happen was an intense make-out session, I thought, like on the bus.

I hurried out of the house to meet him; I was excited and felt a sense of relief from the pain of losing my grandmother.

I should've turned back the minute I met him. He wasn't excited to see me, and I knew it. He barely said three words to me on the way to my house, but I was so desperate for him to see me that I did everything possible to make sure the walk was pleasant.

At the house, he became charming, kind and soft. As we sat on my grandmother's old light-brown couch, which she had passed down to my mother, he leaned in to kiss me. It felt safe, I was in control … until he asked to go to my bedroom. That's the first time I recognised a bad feeling in my gut. Reluctantly, I agreed. We sat on my bed, I in my well-worn pink underwear with yellow polka dots. He asked if we could do it, and I said, 'No.' There was no kicking, no screaming, no violence. No tears. Just a single frightened *no*.

Before I knew it he was inside me, pursuing his own pleasure. As I lay staring up at my ceiling waiting for him to finish, the excruciating pain of having my virginity broken was numbed by my mind running wild. What if I fall pregnant? What if I get AIDS? I had been saving myself for my marriage. What if my mom finds out? Am I already pregnant? Am I sick? Am I dirty? Does he love me now? And finally: am I going to hell?

What took a few minutes felt like hours. I had to accept that what defined me as a pure woman was now gone. As soon as he finished, he jumped up and asked me to walk him halfway home, as though what he had just done was nothing. This time, the roles were reversed: I was silent and he was giddy. Everything my mother had ever said to me on this subject rushed through my brain, and I knew I had sinned. Not once did it occur to me that I had been date-raped, only that I had had sex before marriage.

I immediately called my older sister in a panic. A part of me hoped she would say there was nothing to worry about, but she called my mother. At the time I felt betrayed. But he ejaculated inside me, and I was four years into puberty. If Tunky hadn't made that call, I could now have a 16-year-old child.

When my parents returned home that night, I wondered if they could tell what had happened. But they revealed nothing until the next afternoon. With tears running down her face, my mother hit me with a belt. That was the last hiding I ever got.

She didn't know I had been raped. All she knew was that her adolescent daughter had had sex, and she responded in the way she thought she had to. The best thing she did for me was take me to the doctor. I was too humiliated to pay attention, but I was probably given a morning-after pill and something to prevent an infection.

In those moments, I felt the love of a mother, the disappointment I had caused her and the anger she felt – all at once. Shame became a part of my personality. To dress it up, I would over-perform in everything, trying to make my parents proud even if it killed me. I also tried hard to be a child once more, but those innocent, carefree days were gone forever.

I never sat at the back of the bus again.

During lockdown, a conversation started about whether young girls should date older guys. As I thought about it, I felt trauma creeping back into my body. A shiver ran down my spine as I remembered what dating an older person in my immaturity had done to me. I did a video on it, and called my mother. For the first time, we discussed what had happened. She apologised, we cried and the shame was lifted.

After 12 years of carrying a burden that wasn't mine, God gently lifted it off me and helped many other women too. Having watched that video, many women wrote to me, thanking me for articulating what had happened to them; a few men also let me know that they recognised what they had done.

That alone has been worth my sharing my journey.

Let me reiterate: I don't share my story because I find it easy or fun, my job is to give permission to heal.

Permission to recognise what happened to you.

Permission to confront patterns in your past and permission to forgive.

My collision with sexual abuse did not start there. I recognised this during Speak Life September 2023. As I facilitated this healing course, my own trauma came knocking on my door once again. My brain had washed it and packed it away, but the body never forgets; at some point, whatever has happened to you will come back begging to be released.

I knew it was time to talk about it when my sister said, 'Me too.'

I was excited about a session I had with a recovery counsellor, Aunt Gail. Over 1 000 attendees joined us on Zoom to talk about healing. Aunt Gail started the session with prayer and guidance. Seated in my office with my library in the background, wearing my soft pink Wisdom & Wellness jersey, I beamed with joy as I anticipated her words reaching so many. (I didn't count myself among them.) The questions poured in, and she responded to each one with love and care.

Like a razor gently slicing a finger, her words cut into my heart: 'Many of us have been molested and we don't even know it.'

When she began to describe what molestation looks like, I knew God was talking to me. My brain in survival mode, I continued the session and wrapped it up with gratitude. Then I went cold. Cold as ice. I ran a bath, filled it with bath salts and vanilla-scented bubble bath, lit my Jo Malone candle and soaked. And called my sister.

'I need to tell you something I've never told anyone.'

'Okay, I'm listening.'

'When I was a kid, he used to play a game with me. It didn't hurt, sometimes it felt good. He was close to the family, and I loved him.'

'He even had a name for the game, right?'

'Yes. Yes ... but how do you know?'

'Because he played it with me too.'

Me too.

At that moment, I broke. I was 29, my sister was 25. We had both had the same experience, as children, that we would discuss only several years later.

Here's the thing about being molested at a young age: it's usually someone with close ties who grooms you. Aunt Gail mentioned how normal it is for the body to enjoy it. As an adolescent, you have no language for that, and you feel confused. I loved this person and I know they loved me too, yet there were moments when they did inappropriate things, but things that felt good. The shame came later, when I told Pinks.

We were at a huge family gathering at my grandmother's home in KZN. Pinks was older, more mature. The night was dark, the stars were bright and the wind was refreshing. As we stood behind the house, I asked with innocent eagerness, 'Does he also play this game with you?' She didn't answer; her look was enough to let me know that what was happening was wrong. Shame washed over me.

The year 2023 would be a year of healing, God had told me. I always go into a time of reflection and prayer to hear what God wants from me in a season, how to channel my work, my attitude, my prayers and my life. And He said healing. I knew it would be messy; I just didn't know how messy.

I found myself questioning my entire existence. My life felt like it was patched together to make it work but the damage had never been examined, just covered over. So, with the help of my therapist, I ripped the bandages off and treated my wounds. It was tough, it hurt and it didn't feel like healing, only pain and suffering. But then …

A few days after Christmas, Brenden and I had a major disagreement, one of those seven-year itch ones that have you packing your bags. Well, I packed an overnight bag, and told him I was going to visit my parents and rest.

The next morning, I came upon my mom and Uncle Jack having an intense conversation. I joined in, and before long so did Nonto and my dad. Let me tell you something: if you ask for my opinion or advice, prepare to hear the truth in its rawest form. I'm not good at surface-level stuff; I prefer speaking and hearing the truth – it helps me to grow and to identify my blind spots. In our family, my mom and I are adept at expressing our feelings; my dad, sister and brother not so much. But on that hot December day, the five of us shared vulnerable parts of ourselves with one another, and finally my sister and I had the courage to tell our parents what had happened all those years before.

My therapist had warned me about the different responses I could get to sharing this information. And we survivors carry the shame of the question: what if they don't believe me? But our parents heard us, believed us and supported us. I had expected nothing less, and it was enough.

REFLECTION

Once we know that those closest to us hold space for us, everything feels lighter. During those hours of vulnerability with my family, I felt God's healing hand gently brush away the fear and shame I had carried from childhood. I was finally free. I just had to speak, and you can too.

Are you a survivor of sexual assault or coercion?
- If so, cast your mind back to that time, to the shame you felt then and perhaps still feel, and put your arms around the person that you were. Tell them the shame is not theirs to bear.
- Now send the shame to its rightful owner. Perhaps you feel ready to confront them directly. Perhaps you'd like to write a letter. It might be a letter you never send, but tell them what their actions did to you.

23

No is
a complete
sentence

I'm not sure if the term 'boundaries' was always in my vocabulary, but I am almost certain that boundaries became a thing for me when my daughter was born.

After everything I had been through, and being a firstborn daughter, I wanted to protect my firstborn daughter a little more. Firstborn girls are subject to expectation and pressure, a pressure I didn't want Nuri to experience.

But setting boundaries is easier said than done.

I have never been a person to do something I don't want to do, but I've always struggled with saying no. In the past, I would come up with a white lie instead. The concept of no being a complete sentence was foreign to me.

Growing up in a black family, most times kids have no say, and adults can kiss them when they feel like it, send them on errands, say what they like to them and about them – the hierarchy is very clear. Similarly, with my first pregnancy, relatives touched my belly, told me what I should be eating and drinking and what I should call my baby, and discussed my appearance. I knew I had to put my newly enlarged foot down.

The first clear boundary I set, with both my mothers, was that no child of mine would have gripe water. Second on my list was that nobody would kiss the child without the child's permission. My grandparents really struggled with this. For as long as I can remember, I have greeted my grandmother and grandfather with a kiss and a hug. You might think my children would do the same. On the contrary, they said no the minute they could utter the word. This beginning of boundary setting was tense and uncomfortable. My children were seen as being disrespectful, but we had to stick with that discomfort.

What I was teaching my babies is that not even their mom and dad could deny their no (or yes, as the case may be), and they never had to explain it.

These days we, and other parents, want to teach children to be confident in saying no should sexual danger loom. We want them to be self-assured in dealing with pressure from friends, and we also want them to be firm in refusing to do or say something that goes against their beliefs, right?

But it starts with us. Do we accept their response? Do we respect it?

If we don't, they won't have the courage to stand up for themselves with others.

Learning to respect Nuri's refusal was more challenging than teaching Zani, who seemed to instinctively know that his refusal was valid. Through this, I began to establish boundaries in my life. At first, they felt restrictive and painful, but as time passed, I realised that boundaries are meant to protect both myself and others.

People who lack boundaries tend not to recognise, respect and honour other people's boundaries. For some, receiving a no can feel like rejection or a personal attack. It's important to remember that it's not.

Boundaries help us to show up better for ourselves and others. A boundary is not a wall that shuts everybody out, it is a fence that sets parameters of protection. There is a polite way, I believe, to establish boundaries. We can set them without apologising or over-explaining, and by being firm.

I learnt to be prepared for various types of responses, and came to understand that how others respond is not a reflection of me or my boundaries. Remember, we are not entitled to receive a positive response from others, but we do have control over our own actions and reactions. Breaking a boundary because the person involved doesn't understand it is harmful to me. It is reinforcing that I am not worthy of making sound decisions to honour myself.

Coming from a place of people-pleasing or familial hierarchy, boundaries take practice. With each no or yes, I grew more comfortable trusting myself.

I don't believe in cancel culture or cutting people off; however, I believe in placing people where they belong in your life. Some people should be loved from afar, and others from close. People who love and care about you will learn to recognise and honour your boundaries.

When I chose to close my office and transition my business to a fully remote setup, my decision was influenced by my role as a mother and the type of leader I strive to become. As I continue to create the kind of work culture I want for my business, I always bear in mind that work is never life or death. If I have to decide between attending my child's swimming gala and starting work at

9 am, I choose my child. And I expect my team to do the same. At first, I was nervous about potentially encouraging a lazy work environment, and being seen as an ineffective leader who doesn't take her work seriously. But it has had the opposite effect. I have managed to build a dedicated, passionate and energetic team who get things done on time. Some members work better in the middle of the night, others prefer early mornings (like me). The work always gets done because we are holistically driven rather than deadline driven.

I also learnt that with boundaries come responsibilities. I do work on weekends and holidays; I have speaking engagements on most Saturday mornings. But most of my Fridays belong to my children. I hardly ever open my laptop on that day. I go to Pilates, have breakfast with my husband and go swimming or have 'ice cream Friday' with my children. The most work I do is check our WhatsApp groups. I take my laptop on holiday, and I work an hour every morning.

Essentially, I have created an environment that allows me to thrive in my work without missing out on being a wife and a mother.

In the early years of our marriage, Brenden and I had multiple conversations about our boundaries and where we stand on various things. Our upbringings have informed our boundaries, and we have had to avoid imposing our preferences on each other. Instead, we offer support and respect, and make adjustments.

My parents attended most of my sports days, and I felt seen. I didn't like it when they could not be there, but I respected it and never questioned my importance. With their work and the travelling distances, Brenden's parents were unable to attend his games. It affected his sense of self-worth. For him, showing up for the children takes a different level of priority than it does for me. While I have missed a few mothers' coffee mornings at the cafeteria, I have never missed a sports day or play. I show up not out of a sense of guilt or a desire to prove my worth as a mother, I am there because it's more important to me to honour my children's plays and sports days than anything else in my diary. My family knows that I cannot always be present but they also know that when I am present, I am there with enthusiasm and a big smile. I am there not because I have to be but because I want to be.

I grew up around strong working women. My grandmother and my mother have always worked, had social lives and served their communities. Even after retiring, my grandmother went back to teach Grade 1 learners isiZulu at my previous primary school. Perhaps they didn't have as much help as I do, but they have always had some form of help.

I believe in having help. When I'm ill, or overwhelmed, Brenden creates adventures for the children, and I explain to them that I am not feeling well. Nuri orders me to bed, and insists that if I get up I stay a few metres away from her; Zani doesn't care about the germs and comes to me for cuddles, which means that most times we both end up ill. I once asked the kids to pray for me. This was their prayer: 'Father Jesus, please make Mommy well so she can watch us swim and we can bake.' Ha!

If Brenden is not available, my mom is happy to take over. There is also our helper, who has been with us since Nuri was born, six years ago.

I know as mothers, we want to present a picture of ourselves as continually cheerful, well and brimming with energy. But as I realised a long time ago, I can't keep that up. Instead of being miserable trying to pretend, Brenden and I have created a home of emotions. Emotions are meant to be felt. We don't always deal well with each other's feelings but, most days, we know that they are healthy and safe.

I probably struggle the most when the children are grumpy or my husband is ill, because I go into fixer mode. I find it difficult to sit with another person's pain or sadness without trying to address it or cheer them up or send them to the doctor. My solution-driven approach works in my business, but when it comes to just letting pain be, I suck. When my daughter complains, I worry that she will grow up to be ungrateful and pessimistic. When my son throws a tantrum, I fear that he will grow up to be filled with rage. When my husband is feeling down, I fear that I will have to become the sole manager in our house. I seem unable to consider it just a bad day or a bad moment; I always think of the worst-case scenario and try to solve it before it gets out of hand.

That's what's happening in my inner world, but to my loved one it can feel as though I lack empathy. And they are right. What keeps me going when I should give up is the same thing that makes me so hard on myself. So, yeah, my emotional boundaries need a bit of work.

Luckily, I am not often ill. I'd like to think it's because I take care of my body and go to therapy. Perhaps I'm also blessed with a strong immune system. Once or twice a year I get hit by a bad dose of flu, my body calling time out from stress. I know this because it happens only when I am struggling to deal with pressure, or I ignore it. I get a tension headache and within a day I'm in bed.

I will not work when I am ill. This hasn't always been the case. In 2021, I was either recovering from flu or getting some new virus; it just never stopped. I medicated and kept going until my body shut down. These days, if I fall ill on a weekday, I get up early as usual, take a shower, make my bed, have breakfast, medicate, and in fresh pyjamas jump straight back into bed. And I stay there until I am well. If I'm preparing for my festival, I nap and work on my laptop every two hours, but for the most part I leave the work to my team. Like I said, I only got to this boundary because I have burnt out and crashed before.

REFLECTION

It's not always easy to understand what a boundary is. Lord knows, I have struggled with even the idea of it. But to me, boundaries are simply about learning to say no, and doing it politely but firmly.

No. It's a full sentence, no explanation necessary.

- Do you implement boundaries?
- Do you find it easy or difficult to do?
- What are non-negotiable boundaries for you with regard to:
  o your body?
  o your child or children?
  o work?
  o money?
- Write it down.
- Practise saying no without making an excuse. Do it courteously, without showing anger or frustration.

  Start with the little things, such as *No, I can't make Sunday lunch* or *No, I can't be on the parents' committee at school*, and then move on to the bigger things.

24

A sign of abundance

I grew up being called stingy. It made me feel insecure and I became hyper-vigilant about it. It led me to set a goal of becoming a more generous person.

Early in our marriage, Brenden and I decided that we would always pay the bill, have enough room in our home for everyone, host Christmas without asking for contributions and be faithful givers at church. These values have become second nature to us.

I don't mind paying for everything; it gives me joy, until I feel used. Then I say, 'No, not any more.' My boundaries with regard to money are strong. I don't mind lending money, but I always lend an amount I can afford to let go of should the person be unable to pay me back. And once a person doesn't pay, that's it – I don't lend them money again.

When the article about my making my first million at age 27 came out, I was surprised that my 'by the way' statement was used as the headline. I don't do many interviews partly for that reason: I talk too much, and interviewers know what sells. A guy I know from back home tweeted, 'Mpoomy, are you not scared of SARS?' I wasn't – I had an accountant to handle my finances by then. But the question prompted one of my own, to myself: should I not have said that?

But I give permission to heal. How can I do that without being transparent?

You may be thinking, 'What does making a million bucks at 27 have to do with healing?'

Well, exactly that … We need to heal our mindset when it comes to money and abundance.

When I got the call about that seven-figure deal, I couldn't believe it. My salon was doing exceptionally well, I had other sources of income, so this deal was the cherry on top. I called my mother. We both gasped into the phone, and I asked her how much I should give to my dad as a thank-you for the seed he had sown in my business and for believing in me. Of course, he wouldn't accept a cent, but that's the primary principle I live by when it comes to money: first fruits. With every new business or extraordinary opportunity, I give first fruits to my parents, and with every single amount that hits my account, I give my tithes to the church. That's ten per cent of my gross income. Then there are the other ways in which I share what I have.

Guided by my grey strands, I have always believed I was meant to be wealthy. I've always imagined myself as prosperous and thriving, which is why I got my first job at such a young age. The idea of asking others for money did not sit well with me; financial independence and the options money offers have been an ongoing priority. I'm not big on superstitions or tales, but this is one that I have always had, and it's proving to be true. At 30, I have a full head of grey hair.

I got my first grey hair at the age of 12. My hair was beautiful –
long, silky and relaxed. I wore it in a low pony on most days if
I wasn't trying to style it like a white girl *sigh*. The things we
went through as young girls … imagine trying to have my overly
moisturised and greasy hair wave like Caucasian hair?

The bell ending first break had just rung and we were all
lined up outside class. Everyone gathered around me, looking in
horrified fascination at this single thread of grey hair. The boys
joked about it, some girls offered to get rid of it. Insecure as I
might have felt inside, I pretended to like it. Nobody was going
to pull that grey hair out!

It was a different story when I got home. I begged my mother
to buy my first box of Inecto dye. Having got his first grey hair
at 21, my dad tried to convince me that this was a sign of luck,
which he had too.

Seeing the grey strand, MaNdlovu gasped with joy and excitement. 'You are going to be rich!' She said it with so much
belief and in the deepest Zulu you can imagine. 'You are so
lucky, so blessed, you are going to be rich, wee Nobelungu,' and
I believed her.

If my grey hair was a sign of wealth, I was going to believe it.
Before I knew it, I had two grey hairs and then a small patch, and
now I have a massive white patch in the front of my hair. I did dye
it a couple of times in primary school, only for it to turn bronze
and wiry. Nowadays people ask me if I have highlighted my hair.

I haven't; it's a sign of my wealth.

So, I walked around really believing that I was born to be
wealthy and a leader, because my grandmother said I would be.
Somehow that belief has worked for me. I don't remember being
broke to the point of desperation. There have been times when
my cash flow was not as comfortable as I would've liked, such as

when I dropped out of university. As a newlywed, I wasn't earning as much as I wanted to. But I have always found a way to make money. I rejected the idea that I could be without it, and money has followed me.

My grandmother replaced an insecurity in me about my hair with her spoken words and deep belief. With this foundation, I have dedicated myself to studying the principles of money, in the Bible, in books and in following financial experts – those who are wealthy, and have financial freedom, an abundance mindset and a generous spirit. Not the ones who ask you to give up your daily coffee, no thank you.

So, yes, I made my first million at 27. How? A combination of the belief I have held for several years, a work ethic that I have had since my first job at 11, having a generous hand (if I get R10 I give R1 back to God; of that million, R100 000 went back to God) and opportunity. Not all of us will make that at 27, but it doesn't mean we can't. It just might not be your benchmark. Comparison is the thief of joy is not just a saying – it's true.

I am relating this because I want to give you permission to let go of the idea that money is evil, or that there is not enough of it. I want you to let go of stinginess, of holding on to money because you believe it will run out. If that's how you treat it, that's what will happen. I am not oblivious to economic conditions and people's different backgrounds. But the press and social media do an effective job of presenting all the bad news about money, which is not taking us anywhere.

I want to unlock the abundance mindset.

Money allows us – women in particular – freedom. Freedom to take control of our lives, to take care of ourselves and our children, to support our family, to never have to ask someone else if we can buy that cup of coffee or that shirt, and to leave relationships that are not aligned with our purposes, God-given or otherwise.

Money is an effective tool to grow our careers, our passions and anything else that is meaningful to us. Money is meant to circulate, not stagnate.

Religion has done a good job of keeping us poor. That's if you have not taken the time to get to know God for yourself. There's having a relationship with God, and then there's religion, where you follow all the rules and in that way live a crippled life. I would like to offer you a relationship where you get to know God for yourself. In doing this for myself, I realised that He is a God of abundance and principle. It is my birthright to be wealthy, but it is my responsibility to access, grow and sustain that wealth. I could quote a number of verses that speak of His abundant hand, but the Book of Proverbs alone is an excellent starting point. Would you believe me if I told you that the Book of Proverbs is one of the best business books ever? If we apply just a fraction of Proverbs, our lives will be transformed.

I suggest that you take a moment to step out into nature, preferably a place where there are lots of trees. Look around and listen. Listen to the birds, focus on the details of the clouds, look closely at each tree. If you are on a beach, gaze at the water, examine the grains of the sand. Do you see? Everything is filled with abundance. Nature is the closest thing to God's original idea for each of us. The sea doesn't run out, the birds don't worry about tomorrow, the sun rises every morning without fail. It is God's nature to make everything unique, beautiful and bountiful. You are part of His ecosystem.

You only have to believe this and tap into it.

Perhaps I sound like I am talking from a position of privilege.

I hope that from what you have read about my story so far, you realise that that's not the case. I have seen that a scarcity mindset keeps people stuck. Let's do away with it. Put aside what doesn't resonate and keep what is in alignment. I talk from having taken this journey, not from being born with a silver spoon in my mouth.

The only silver I was born with was in my hair.

REFLECTION

As a highly therapised black girl, I've picked up a thing or two over the years. Firstly, money is spiritual, and secondly, we all have a relationship with money.

Cast your mind back to when you were growing up ...
- What beliefs did you have about money?
- Were they helpful thoughts? Or were you brought up with a scarcity mindset?
- What do you wish you had been taught about money?
- How can you change negative patterns of thinking about money? What will you say to that negative voice in your head?
- Write it all down.

A sign of abundance

25

Failure, real and imagined

Money has made my life easier, but it hasn't all been plain sailing.

On my journey to 30, there have been many detours and bumps in the road. I find it difficult to call these bumps failures because I don't identify with failure, at least in the traditional sense. My optimistic nature always has me believing that it was just never meant to be.

A vivid moment of extreme disappointment occurred in 2022. I had been nominated for the *Forbes* 30 Under 30. This was not just a dream of mine but a goal I set out to achieve in order to prove my success, to prove that dropping out of varsity was not a mistake but a directive from God. I did everything possible to adequately apply and prove why I was worthy of making the list. My friend Candice, a brilliant writer, agreed to help me write up my profile and gather my achievements. After a brief catch-up and coffee, we put our heads down. I prayed, I felt confident; I believed I was walking in my miracle. God was answering the prayer I had made years before.

Still, I kept checking my emails, operating from a place of uncertainty even though my lips said otherwise. Many of us self-sabotage, we suffocate our dreams by not trusting that whatever the outcome, it is the one meant to be.

To confirm my confidence, I was invited to Botswana for the *Forbes* event and advised to prepare for a photoshoot. They emphasised that this didn't mean I was chosen, but it felt pretty real to me. I went to Botswana with outfits, a makeup artist booked, the works. But when I got there, I realised I hadn't made it when my makeup artist mentioned having done the makeup for an earlier shoot. Hoping that there was still a chance, I kept checking my emails. On the day the list came out, I got my answer: no. I was shattered and humiliated.

Perhaps that's how I would describe failure: I was humiliated because I had shared my dreams. So confident that it was happening, I did what I don't usually do and blurted it out to anyone who would listen. I told my dear friend Amanda that if I got on *Forbes*, I would have a black-tie dinner to celebrate. She suggested I have it even if I didn't make it – being on the shortlist was enough. But that's not how I view things. That afternoon, in the corner of my living room with rain streaming against the windows, I sat on the floor and wept. In true Brenden style, my husband held me and assured me that they, not me, were the problem. It wasn't actually the case, but he says things like that to make me feel better about myself.

I spent that whole weekend crying, eating and watching *The Fixer.*

I did make the *Forbes* 30 Under 30 the following year, having reluctantly applied after receiving another nomination. Correction: Brenden pushed me to apply. And, as you may have guessed,

I didn't commemorate it. The black-tie dinner never happened.

I was thrilled, I exhaled and I shared the news on my social media platforms. Another thing was ticked off my list. But our home had just been flooded, and I had very little room to celebrate.

It's crazy how opposing things can be true at the same time. On the one hand, I had just hosted my first successful event with over 1 000 people, appeared on the cover of a magazine, been to Bali with my husband and was a *Forbes* 30 Under 30; on the other hand, our home was ruined. I didn't know how to feel. Should I feel grateful because at least we had the means to fix it, and so much good was happening in our lives, or should I mourn the loss and heartbreak?

Many of us find ourselves in this place, where suddenly our dreams are coming true after a long period of struggle. We are living in answered prayers, yet we are partly aching in disbelief at how we can feel so much gratitude and pain at the same time. We tend to try to minimise our pain in an effort to show our gratitude, but that is a recipe for disaster.

Most times, I treat disappointment as a path to something bigger and better. I stand by this, but feelings are just as important. They are meant to be felt, not brushed away by toxic positivity.

REFLECTION

Failure may not always be welcome, but if we embrace it, it makes a brilliant teacher.

But you're never going to win unless you try, and sometimes when you try you lose. Look at the great example of Brené Brown's daughter coming last in a swimming race. She gets lapped, she is in tears but she finishes the race. Sometimes that is all we can do:

finish the race even though we're coming last.

- Name three things you've failed at.
- What did those failures teach you?
- Have you learnt more from your failures than from your successes?
- Do you fear failure? If so, what would you do with your life if you didn't?
- Write it down.

26

Sorry,
not sorry

A while ago, I invited my husband to go for an afternoon drive. It had been a hectic week, and I just wanted to spend some time with him outside the house. Did that man not collect the entire household and squeeze us into his little Abarth?

At this point my children are almost six and almost four. Zani grows with each breath, so every drive has become a shopping trip for shoes and clothes that fit. And if you have children, you know how messy a shopping trip can be. The good news is that the children asked Brenden to take them to a bookshop, and my clenched jaw relaxed. At the shop, my gaze landed on a book called *Girl, Stop Apologizing* by Rachel Hollis. I opened it and this jumped out at me: sorry, not sorry.

After reading that book, I started listing things that I am no longer apologising for. And, fam, I suggest you do the same, even if you come up with just one thing. As you step into your power, you may find that many people are upset with you for that, and that's when your list of sorry, not sorry will start growing.

Here is my list:

1. I have big dreams. These dreams require focus, excellence and discipline. I have proven to myself that I am worthy of them; I show up as that person, and I'm equipped to be that person. My life, relationships and everything else would be simpler if I toned it down a bit, but that's not who I am. So, sorry, not sorry.

2. I am needy. That funny video about being an emotional gangster? That's me! I love showing up at my full power but I also love a soft landing. I will drive two hours to lie on my parents' couch while my dad makes me coffee, my mom plays with my toes, I cuddle my sister's baby and we talk. Quality time, physical touch, acts of service and emotional safety, all combined.

3. I want to look good. My mother is aging like fine wine, and I plan to do the same. And when you look good, you feel good.

4. I love the finer things in life, and I don't mind doing the work. My expectations when it comes to flights, hotel rooms and the kind of coffee I drink might be on the more luxurious side, but it gets me up at 5 am.

5. I struggle to do one thing at a time. My brain is always in a buzz. No matter how hard I try not to, at least five projects are running in my head. I'm in a continual state of anxiety about finishing the unfinished things. While I'm busy with one thing, I will leave it to do another thing that just popped up. I would love to be laser-focused, but then again, I feel like multitasking is my superpower.

6. I'm not a dog person. I have tried having a dog but am too much of a perfectionist for that. I hate poop in my garden, I don't enjoy my things being chewed. I am a plant mom.

I love trees, lavender bushes and hydrangeas. When my dog pulled my hydrangeas out, my lack of understanding led me to realise that I am a better aunt to my sister's dogs than a dog owner. It made me sad, but it's true, and I like truth more.

7. I am an introvert. My year of 2023 taught me that. I need time alone to feel safe and to feel like myself. I have amazing quality time by myself. I gladly open up and give of myself to others, but time alone is something I won't compromise on.

8. I am stopping … I have not stopped yet, but I am stopping apologising for having boundaries. Each successful woman I have studied has boundaries. They may make the people around her uncomfortable, but she gets to show up as the healthiest version of herself, and all who love and know her appreciate those boundaries. Boundaries have saved me. If I didn't have them, my life would look a lot different.

9. I can't connect with deceitful people. I made the decision to live an honest and vulnerable life. Where there is lying and pretence, I cringe. I will slip out of any conversation with a dishonest person. And I don't want perfect people around me; I want honest people so I can be free to be honest. Lies make me dizzy.

10. I don't fit in. I'm a weirdo and that's fine; there are moments when I let that freak flag fly. Sorry, not sorry.

REFLECTION

Now it's your turn. Let me remind you that you are lovable, capable and unique just as you are, and you don't have to apologise for that.

- What are you not sorry for?
- Make a list. Write it down.

27

What I love most

The American spiritual teacher and author Gary Zukav talks about a spiritual partnership being a partnership between equals, for the purpose of spiritual growth. That idea changed how I view my husband. We are spiritual partners, and that means we challenge each other. In 2023 I almost called it quits because it was just too hard, but it was also the year I knew that I really love this guy.

My husband is a beautiful, kind, soft and passionate man. A genius of note and the most selfless person I know. A fighter for and protector of what he loves. The passion that drew me to him is the passion that challenges me. If it weren't for Brenden, I wouldn't have followed most of my dreams. He gave me the courage to follow my heart and figure the rest out later. He still does. I am calculating, he is driven by the heart; together, our combination is potent.

Brenden is the kind of person who sacrifices for others. After I had dropped out of university and was feeling very low, he was there for me. He had just signed a new record deal and was meant to fly to Durban to work with a producer. He chose to drive there instead, so that I could accompany him and not be alone during that dark time. On the night of his session, I got a call for an audition. I was ready to forfeit it but he insisted that we return the next day. His belief in me made me believe in me, and I got the role.

That audition was the glimpse of hope I needed in order to show me that I would be okay. In Brenden, I met someone to whom God whispered His plans for my life and someone who carried the strength and courage to marry a woman like me. Together, we challenge toxic masculinity, and culture and traditions that make no sense. We live honestly, even if it makes others uncomfortable.

My husband excels at putting himself in my shoes. I'm a tough cookie but he can reach parts of me nobody else can. The parts that I have protected.

I love how he fathers our children. His childlike spirit comes alive when he is with them, especially our daughter. He makes them tea and the best ham and cheese sandwiches (according to them). He has taught them everything he knows about Formula 1, soccer and PlayStation.

I love his general knowledge. He knows everything about everything. If you need to make a good impression, he is the guy to take with you.

I love that he lets me be me. In a culture that has always and still continues to suppress women, he is aware of my gift and my life's calling. He understands what comes with it, and no matter how challenging and difficult it is, he is the first to cheer me on. He sees things nobody else can see, he hears elements of a song that make it an instant hit, he starts the first sentence for my speaking engagements and has me writing like a poet. He is a creative genius.

As for my family … God really does give you the family that you need. I look at other families and think, 'All hell would've broken loose if I was there,' but then I look at my family and think, 'Nobody else would stand for this.' But I love them. I love how different everybody is and at the same time so accepting of one another.

My mother creates a safe space for everyone, her arms always open for rest, regulation and a whole lot of love. She is passionate about her career but will put everything aside for her grandchildren. She has found the little girl in her, in her 50s. She loves learning new things, colouring in, gardening, taking walks, camping with my dad and going on dates with her girlfriends. Almost every weekend she makes the two-hour journey to be with her grandchildren. I love all that.

My dad has an adventurous spirit. He believes so deeply in himself it sometimes feels like delusion. But he has that same confidence and belief in all of us. He has become softer and more vulnerable with age. He insists on having big birthday parties and a birthday cake to make up for not having them as a child. I love all that.

My siblings are hilarious. All stubborn, and all gifted. Our personalities are very different but when we sit in beautiful moments, we silently find what brings us together. No matter what happens, our family shows up for each other.

My in-laws are kind and loving. The first thing my mother-in-law said to me was 'I love you', and I have seen evidence of that in many ways.

There are days when I come home having faced rejection, and feelings of unworthiness and failure. I walk in hoping just to go to bed. Then I hear two voices screaming 'Mommy' and all the hardness starts melting away. My children don't make everything okay, but they remind me of what matters most. They reach parts of my heart I never knew existed. On Thursdays at 2 pm I take an hour from work to watch them swim, and I am in awe every time. I fully believe my babies are the smartest, most beautiful and most talented children in the world.

Recently, despite her good swimming technique, Nuri didn't trust herself so she held on tightly to her teacher. Despite his questionable kicking technique, Zani confidently dived in before the teacher could even give the word. I had pep talks with each of them, and we practised at home, so the next time we went my girl glided through the water by herself and my boy demonstrated his best kicking and breathing. We are ready for the 2036 Olympics!

The talks I give them when they feel unworthy are also talks to the little girl in me. Our 'ice cream Friday' ritual, when each of us picks our favourite ice cream, is also for little Mpumi and young Brenden, who growing up heard 'I don't have the money' once too often for their liking. Then there are the evening walks and the morning school drops, during which I teach them how to pray and live a grateful life.

For some women, motherhood has taught them to be selfless. By contrast, motherhood has given me the opportunity to get to know myself and take care of myself. Because I am a mother I have a morning routine; there is an hour each day that belongs just to me: I go to gym, I bake. These things make motherhood incredible and my children's lives better, but they have also amplified who I am. They have confirmed that I love the woman I am. I went to therapy only after having my first baby. Motherhood has helped me find myself and on that journey I am helping my babies discover who they are, and what God's path is for them. What a gift.

Of course there are days when I need help, and there are nights when I'd rather skip the bedtime stories because I'm not in the mood for all the questions that follow. But then I do it, and I realise that I love doing it. Motherhood is for me. Not as my mother did it, or as others said it should be; my babies and I have found our own rhythm. When it stops working we go back to the drawing board and make room for our growth, changes and seasons, and are soon in flow again.

I watch my daughter and I thank God that I am a woman. That little girl's intuition shocks me every time. She sees things nobody else can see, she trusts her gut so much it scares me, and when something doesn't feel right to her, her entire body changes. She feels deeply and cares about things nobody taught her to care about. Her future is very clear in her mind, and every day I see her joyfully do things that confirm God's voice. I am her and she is me.

I've often judged myself for taking things too personally or not following the crowd, compromising not even a little. But then Nuri came along, and all the things I was judging myself about I admire and encourage in her. I love being a woman because of my gut feelings. I lead by instinct, in relationships and business. If a situation appears to be a good idea but makes me queasy or uneasy, I know that my gut is sending me a warning. Oprah's grandmother's dream for her was to find a good white family to work for. But she knew deep inside that there was more for her. That's intuition. Womanhood gifted me wisdom; even the Book of Proverbs refers to 'wisdom' as 'her'.

Wisdom is the ability to apply relevant knowledge in an insightful way, a way that is different from that in which the knowledge was gained. Wisdom can also be defined as seeing a situation as God sees it, acting on it as God wills and learning from it as

God intended all along. I may question a lot of things but I never question my wisdom. It informs my ability to collect information and knowledge, my ability to be still and then make decisions that have a lasting impact, and my ability to see beauty in even the most crooked roads.

That's why I love being a woman.

In the Book of Esther, we read about her ability to trust her God-given wisdom to save an entire nation. An act of stupidity would've ended the lives of many, including herself. I value my wisdom more than anything else I possess, and as I share it with others I ask God to help me. I seldom pray for material things; I pray for wisdom because, through wisdom, much can be gained.

I love being a woman because of my nurturing gifts. Growing up, I never offered to babysit or carry someone's child in church, as my sister lovingly did. I preferred running around and keeping busy. I thought something was wrong with me. Later, I realised that my nurturing spirit is different: I nurture dreams.

I am always asking people about their goals, dreams and visions. Once these are clear, I offer help; I offer my resources and my wisdom. I always have, even in the smallest of ways. It took time for me to notice that that in itself is nurturing. Then I had my babies, and the seed of my nurturing spirit blossomed. My entire business ethos is based on nurturing dreams, but I love children too. Not just my own. My friend's children FaceTime me to say goodnight. My sister's son looks at me like nothing else matters. And I am involved in projects where I speak to girls the way I would have loved to be spoken to. I questioned it then but I know it now. If not for her nurturing spirit, the daughter of Pharaoh wouldn't have saved baby Moses from the river. He was safely tucked up and protected in that basket – that too was because of a woman's wisdom and nurturing spirit.

I love being a woman because of my resilience, my ability to fight till the very end, in spite of all that comes against me. Not to forget my body, which communicates emotions I sometimes try to overlook. When I think something doesn't bother me, I feel it in my neck. When a moment is beyond my wildest dreams, the butterflies in my stomach confirm it. And when there's injustice, my heart beats faster. In the wrong environment I get the chills, and whether I am happy, sad or laughing hysterically, I cry. I might not understand my emotions in the moment, but my body will always signal to me. What a gift.

I love being a black woman because I am so brilliant, unique and precious that history has worked over time to try to shut me up. Those who went before me gave themselves up so that my brilliance could give permission to others to tap into theirs. I've always believed that there must be something spectacular about being a black woman, because so many systems were built to suppress her. But that fight is being won, one day at a time. Every day we see headlines of a black woman going against the odds and setting new world standards. Every other day we hear of 'the first black woman to …'. As confirmed by the late great Maya Angelou, against all odds a black woman rises. She doesn't rise alone, she carries many with her and nurtures their dreams until they are ready to flourish.

I love being a black woman.

REFLECTION

Have you ever been in a situation where your gut sent you a signal? No, fam, I'm not talking about how you felt after eating too much ice cream!

- Think about a time when your gut told you not to do something. Did you listen? What was the outcome?
- Write it down.
- Think about a time when your gut told you to do something. Did you listen? What was the outcome?
- Write it down.
- Read what you've written. Are you good at listening to your gut or is this something you need to work on?

What I love most

28

Final word

Writing a memoir, or what I like to call an 'introduction to me', has been a healing process. I've always advocated for therapy, but now I also advocate that everyone writes a book about their life, be it for public consumption or not. In this process I sat through feelings that I used to run from. It has allowed me to acknowledge the beautiful parts of me without trying to cover them up with a but, no … I learnt discipline. Oh my, how I learnt discipline! While I was writing this book, I was also planning a festival, my mother-in-law was battling serious health issues and, with just 24 hours in a day, a lot of sacrifices had to be made.

Writing from 5 to 6 am, some days I could reach the 1 000-word goal I had set myself, some days I managed only 500, and some, when the muse decided to cooperate (she's a feisty thing), I was blessed with over 2 000. I learnt to accept however much I managed to write each day and I learnt to show up even when I really, *really* didn't feel like it. I learnt to honour my body. I took notes on the parts that made me squirm just that little bit more and what triggered me. I learnt that I am trustworthy and committed – something I spent six years working on, and I value it.

Writing helped me forgive; I accepted the apologies I never received, because writing gave me the full perspective of what happened. The process was difficult and there were moments of doubt. Did I have anything valuable to share? Was the time and hard work I was pouring into this worth it? Would anyone even want to read my book? And would I be shamed for my honesty? On those days, I would remind myself that my story was necessary to give others permission to heal.

I believe in co-creating with God, and in that process knowing He will send me both vision and inspiration. A Pinterest board helps me map this out. On a daily basis, I ask myself: what does this type of woman do every day, and how does she show up? I believe in manifesting, in trusting that God has dropped a dream and I get to work with Him to bring it to life. What's meant for me will be mine, I know that. I also know that I need to do my part to access it, to do the inner work to be ready for it.

One of my prayers is 'God, if it's not from you, take my desire away'. This prayer has carried me and my dreams safely time and again. I also believe that each dream and vision is like a baby growing in a womb, not to be shared with and touched by everyone, but to be incubated until it is ready to be birthed.

Dear reader, my hope is that my stories ignite something in you, an impulse to be inquisitive about your own life.

I hope you get to unpack the good and the bad.

I hope you get to change your mind about things that don't serve you.

I hope you get to co-create the life of your dreams with God.

I hope you become familiar with pain and failure, that you don't wish them away but use them as an important tool in this journey called life.

I hope you address the elephant in the room, and forgive.

I hope you awaken the dreamer in you, bearing in mind that life is not meant to be a breeze, it's meant to be lived in all seasons: winter, spring, summer and autumn.

I hope you get to choose the kind of person you want to be (it's so easy to fall in line and never find out who you are).

I hope you celebrate, not in the way you are told to but in your own way.

I hope each book people read is a step towards eliminating cancel culture. We need more grace and kindness, and people's views should not be ignored or discarded.

As we all write our own story, we see parts of us we would rather tuck away, but when we do the work, we are able to navigate life with all its contradictions. I hope you do the work to love yourself so you can love others.

I hope you change the narrative in your environment. It will come with pushback, but when you know your 'why?' you don't stop. You have something the world needs, but the world needs you well so that you can share in love, and not bleed.

Thank you for travelling on this journey with me, one I continue to figure out as I go along. I don't think we ever get to a point where we have it all figured out, but whether you do or not, you will have tried.

Dear reader, I give you permission to *heal*.

FINAL REFLECTION

What do you love about being you ... perfectly imperfect, unique *you*?

- Write down five things you love about yourself.
- Keep it safe and read it every day.

Final final word

I am not a person who lends books, mainly because I write in them. If I encounter a passage that resonates, I have to write a big old 'agreed' in the margin. That's why if someone likes a book, I will buy them their own copy rather than lend them mine. As Pastor TD Jakes points out, you cannot lead if you do not read, so let's create more leaders by creating more readers. We can only do that if people have access to books. Books really do make the best gifts, so buy a copy for yourself and one for a friend, and let's grow the reading culture.

Nothing is better than the smell of a new book!

The reading list

- [ ] *Year of Yes* by Shonda Rhimes
- [ ] *Bamboozled by Jesus: How God Tricked Me into the Life of My Dreams* by Yvonne Orji
- [ ] *What Happened to You? Conversations on Trauma, Resilience, and Healing* by Bruce D Perry and Oprah Winfrey
- [ ] *Girl, Stop Apologizing* by Rachel Hollis
- [ ] *The 5AM Club* by Robin Sharma
- [ ] *The Alchemist* by Paulo Coelho

The soundtrack to my life

♪ 'Free your dreams' – Chantae Cann
♪ 'You're all I need to get by' – Aretha Franklin
♪ 'Immediately' – Tasha Cobbs Leonard
♪ 'Grace' – Tasha Cobbs Leonard
♪ 'Lonely at the top' – Asake & H.E.R.
♪ 'God if its You' – Brenden Praise & Free 2 Wrshp featuring Mpoomy Ledwaba
♪ 'Mountains and molehills' – PJ Morton
♪ 'I will exalt you' – Brooke Fraser
♪ 'Until you come back to me' – Aretha Franklin
♪ 'Somebody's son' – Tiwa Savage featuring Brandy
♪ 'Seasons' – Madison Ryann Ward
♪ 'Sugarcane remix' – Camidoh featuring Mayorkun, King Promise and Darkoo
♪ 'Singayaphi uma sisuka kuwe' – Jumbo
♪ 'Ngegama lakho Nkosi' – Ncandweni Christ Ambassadors
♪ 'Horns in the sun' – DJ Kent featuring Mo-T, Mörda and Brenden Praise

Acknowledgements

I look at my world, and I am in awe of all the angels on earth who have extended their lives, their wisdom and their time to ensure my commitment to my course.

To my loving Father, the one who knew me before I was formed and chose me, knowing all my complexities, thank you for wisdom, lessons, and, above all, love. My beautiful husband, Brenden, thank you for co-creating with me, dashing to the garage to get me salted caramel ice cream and rainbow puffs when I need them most, brilliantly lending me a few sentences for my book, and being a mirror. In all seasons, God continues to keep us. I am blessed to call you friend, baby daddy, love of my life, head of our home, and my husband.

To my publisher, Sibongile, your unwavering belief in my story, even when I doubted that I had anything to say, has been a source of strength. Our conversation started almost four years ago, and I've run away from you more times than I can count, but your dedication, passion and delicacy for human stories are the wings every first-time author needs. To Zwanga, who was the first to court me from Jonathan Ball Publishers, I often joke that you sealed the deal long before the conversation was had; you and the marketing team and the rest of the family at JBP have held my hand through the last 12 months and believed in me more than I believed in myself – thank you.

My incredible team at Wisdom & Wellness, our shared journey, marked by passion, creativity, diligence and sensitivity, has been a testament to our unity. Through tears, laughter, exhaustion, thrill, deadlines and passion, we have done it together. Thank you for being part of this journey.

To my parents, siblings, my friends and family, you are the foundation upon which I stand. Your love, support and guidance have shaped me into the person I am today. I am forever grateful for your presence in my life.

My beautiful boy Zani, whose morning cuddles kept Mommy going when I had nothing else to write. To be needed by you has given my life so much meaning and purpose. My little big boy, your quick pop-ins while I was writing gave me the extra push I needed. My Nuri girl, your curiosity and determination have taught me more about myself than anything else. Thank you, my babies, for loving Mommy unconditionally

My aunt Gail and my friend Amanda, you know parts of me nobody will ever know, and yet you have held me tighter and loved me harder. There is no book without you two. You have each carried me in prayer and words of wisdom, covered me when I felt naked and sheltered me when I just needed to sleep. You continue to release me from my own prison of perfectionism and spoil me with love and care. Thank you.

Last but not least, my community. Your unwavering support has been the backbone of every endeavour I have embarked on, from the nail bar to opening a salon, then a YouTube channel, all my content, my podcast, the big and small events, responding to my Sunday emails and now being part of my book. Your presence has filled my heart with gratitude and joy.

Piecing these words together has been a journey of tears, rec-onciliation, love and answering some really important questions. This book has gifted me the opportunity to sit back, slow down and search for the meaning of my life now. Outside of the accom-plishments, the need to achieve, the proving a point, who am I? And while I journey with God, I pray that you receive the gift to change your mind, slow down and know that you are worthy just because you are you!

Life is beautiful in all its complexities, and it is meant to be savoured, not rushed. I am learning that now, and who knows what this next decade looks like? I am just glad I finally know that I have nothing to prove; I can just be.

To little Nompumelelo, you, baby girl, are enough.